ELEVATE YOUR SUCCESS

ELEVATE YOUR SUCCESS

THE MOST INSPIRING WAY TO TAKE YOUR SUCCESS TO THE NEXT LEVEL

Foreword by Dr John Demartini
Human Behaviour Specialist, Educator & Teacher From "The Secret"

Disclaimer

All the information, techniques, skills and concepts contained within this publication are of the nature of general comment only and are not in any way recommended as individual advice. The intent is to offer a variety of information to provide a wider range of choices now and in the future, recognising that we all have widely diverse circumstances and viewpoints.

Should any reader choose to make use of the information contained herein, this is their decision, and the contributors (and their companies), authors and publishers do not assume any responsibilities whatsoever under any condition or circumstances. It is recommended that the reader obtain their own independent advice.

First Edition 2016

Copyright © 2016 by Author Express

All rights reserved. No part of this publication may be reproduced, stored in a retrieval system, or transmitted in any form or by any means, electronic, mechanical, photocopying, recording or otherwise, without the prior written permission from the publisher.

National Library of Australia

Cataloguing-in-Publication entry:

Creator: Harvey, Benjamin J., author.

Other Authors:

Bailey, Nathan | Coe, David | Hartmann, Anna | Jones, Fiona | Moran, Shandra | Lok, Ivor | Ng, Ed | Pich, Samith | Tiong, Kim | Walker, Kim

Title: Elevate Your Success / Benjamin J Harvey.

ISBN: 9781925471038 (paperback)

Subjects:
Success.
Success in business.
Self-actualization (Psychology)

Dewey Number: 650.1

Published by Author Express
From Inspiration to Publication in 5 Simple Steps
www.AuthorExpress.com
publish@authorexpress.com

Dedication

To fellow learners wanting to take their success to the next level. This book is dedicated to you.

Benjamin J Harvey and co-authors

Foreword by Dr John Demartini

You possess seven secret treasures, incredible riches already within you. These relate to the seven areas of your life you can empower: mental, vocational, financial, relationships, social, physical and spiritual. To balance these treasures, or riches, there are also seven fears that stop you on the way to success. These are: fear of failure, fear of rejection, fear of not being smart enough, fear of not being beautiful enough, fear of scarcity, fear of authority and the fear of society's judgements.

The number one reason people don't succeed in a certain area is that they're not living according to their highest values. It's the same reason most New Year's resolutions don't work. They're not aligned with what's truly important to them.

Everyone lives by a set of values, from most important to least important. Your highest values are those you're inspired from within to do spontaneously. As you move down your list of priorities, you require outside motivation to do it. When you set a goal that's aligned to your highest values, you will experience increased confidence, achievement and belief, and will therefore experience more success.

Too many people don't achieve their goals, because they're living according to their lowest values. When you compare yourself to someone else's success, you lose focus and inspiration. When you compare yourself to others and put them on a pedestal, then you're living your life by someone else's values.

Successful people spend their time doing what's highest priority on their list and delegate the lowest priority. Most people buy brands instead of creating brands. They want immediate gratification to feel better about themselves, because they're not living their true, authentic life.

If you're looking for a coach or mentor on your success journey, don't just select the person because they're successful. Select them because they're successful and they have some alignment with your mission and your values.

In my experience, doing what you love and loving what you do is the most powerful way to increase your wealth.

The secret to success is learning to serve. When you help enough people get what they want, you truly make a difference. And if you're grateful for being able to serve, then you, too, will get what you want and *Elevate your Success*.

Dr John F. Demartini
Human Behaviour Specialist
www.DrDemartini.com

BONUS GIFT

The Elevate YOU
7 Day Transformation

Want to take the top 7 areas of your life to the next level?

There is ONE powerful 'Elevate Process' you can use immediately to improve Your Relationships, Health, Finances, Mindset and any other area of your life.

In this transformational 7 day online course, Benjamin J Harvey guides you through the "Elevate Process" and how you can improve your life from the inside-out.

Normally valued at $295
Get FREE and instant access here:

www.elevate-books.com/you

Life Rewards Action. Get started today!

Contents

Prosper From Your Passion — 1
Benjamin J Harvey

Bearfoot Business — 23
Anna Hartmann

CEO YOU — 41
Shandra Moran

The Bandits' Gift — 61
David Coe

Resilience To Brilliance — 79
Kim Walker

Inspired Income — 97
Nathan Bailey

Mind Over Matchsticks — 119
Kim Tiong

Dreams Do Come True — 137
Ivor Lok

Online Success — 159
Samith Pich

PassionPreneur — 179
Fiona Jones

Marketing To Millions — 197
Ed Ng

"Giving yourself permission
to do what you love is the key to
elevating all areas of your life."

~ Benjamin J Harvey

Benjamin J Harvey

Prosper From Your Passion

In his pursuit to assist people in finding the answers to life's most intriguing questions, Benjamin J Harvey has studied the psychology of empowerment for over ten years. Knowing that reading books like the Elevate series empowers people to bring their dreams into reality, Benjamin has been assisting thousands of people across the globe to empower themselves and live abundantly on purpose.

In 2009 he founded Authentic Education with business partner Cham Tang, to help empower people to live abundantly on purpose. As a result, Authentic Education went on to achieve something that has never been done before in the history of personal development. They received the BRW Fast Starters Award in 2013 and then backed it up in 2015 by being named in the BRW Fast 100 as the thirty-eigth fastest-growing company in Australia.

Benjamin J Harvey

Prosper From Your Passion

How did you start a company teaching others to live their love and get where they are?

Back in 2002 I was coming out of my fifth year of chronic depression. I was unemployed for most of that time, heavily overweight, massively in debt and all of the medication the doctors had me on was doing nothing to change my situation in life.

I decided to get a job in recruitment to get out of debt and out of my house. I wanted to help people live a more fulfilling life, and I thought maybe I could make an impact by getting people jobs they enjoyed. After four years of doing that, I realised I had a big problem on my hands: I wasn't passionate about the industry and therefore was incongruent with my own inner voice.

In 2005 I maxed out my credit card by investing a large amount of money into attending educational seminars on personal development, energy healing, coaching and business, and a whole new world opened up to me.

I was still about $137,000 in debt at the time, but I knew something had to change, and that whatever got me to this point in my life wasn't going to get me any further. I needed to learn something new in order to move forward.

By 2006 I had opened up my own coaching business, left the corporate world and was well on my way to living true to my personal mission of helping people to live abundantly on purpose.

In 2009, Cham Tang, my business partner, and I launched Authentic Education, and over six and a half years later it has impacted the lives of tens of thousands of people across Australia by helping them find effective ways to live their love.

In 2013, Authentic Education was awarded the BRW Fast Starters Award, given out by Business Review Weekly to the top one hundred companies that achieve the fastest business success in the first two-three years of launching.

Just two short years later, Authentic Education backed it up by being awarded the BRW Fast 100 Award, which is given to the top one hundred companies across Australia to achieve the largest year-on year-growth in a specific period of time. Authentic Education was ranked thirty-eighth in Australia.

Receiving both of these awards only two years apart is a feat that has never before been achieved by a company in our industry, and both Cham and I are grateful to have received them due to the incredible success our clients have created in their lives.

So how did we do it? People think that to be successful in business, or life for that matter, they need to take some giant leap from where they are to where they want to be. They often say they want "massive action", but this couldn't be further from the truth.

Success is a process, not an outcome, and to be successful, you must learn to take small actions that build momentum over time, and then continually refine those actions until each one is completed at a world-class level.

Then all you need to do is possess an *until attitude*. This simply means you persist with taking small actions and refining them every step of the way *until* you get there.

Believe it or not, stubbornness is a fantastic trait to have if you want to succeed it in life. Listen to your heart and have the courage to follow your inner voice.

What advice do you have to make a small business a success?

People on a mission have no competition, so get on your mission and start to change the world in some way. You will be glad you did.

Be sure to dedicate your time to that which truly lights you up and makes a difference in the world. Passion is the single most important ingredient when it comes to being successful. Once you have it, you're halfway there.

Anyone can make it in business if they allow themselves to:

- be highly coachable
- find great mentors
- get relevant education
- take little actions and refine those actions
- listen to qualified feedback
- believe in their product

Oh, and always remember: it's not about you. Business is about making the lives of your clients better in some way by solving meaningful problems for them. So stop thinking about yourself and start focussing on changing people's lives.

As Zig Ziglar once said, "You can have everything you want in life if you help other people get what they want."

It sounds like you practice what you preach.

Both Cham and I absolutely love what we do. I feel deeply this is my mission in life, and therefore an exit strategy could not be further from my mind. It's important we preach what we practise, so how can we be teaching people to do what they love if we're not doing it ourselves?

Having said that, I realise that values can change, and you can get bored with what you're doing. Though I see myself in the field of education for at least the next forty years, I will say that you should always run a business as if you're going to sell it one day. Authentic Education has sound business systems set up, should the need ever arise.

I really think there are two types of businesses:

1. Lifestyle

2. Asset

Cham and I definitely feel Authentic Education is a lifestyle business. We see what we do as the ultimate lifestyle for ourselves, our partners, our family and our team members. Of course, we also teach our clients to do the same.

How can someone prosper from their passion?

In order to monetise your passion, I suggest you order and organise what you know and love.

Over the years, money has flowed to where knowledge is most organised. We've left the information age and are entering the knowledge age, so people want to be able to quickly digest the information they're looking for. Human beings are unconsciously attracted to people who have organised knowledge.

You already have information someone else needs and wants, you just have to share it, which most people love to do. This is what a business or organization is: bringing to the market an organised form of that which is disorganised.

In order to make money, it basically comes down to getting your message to the market. Where a lot of people go wrong is thinking the messenger chooses the method by which the message is delivered, but you need to be flexible about this.

An example is if you wanted to write a book. You would be attracted to the person who has that knowledge ordered and organised in a step-by-step process for you to follow. That knowledge can be packaged and then delivered by various methods, such as a book, an online program, workshop, one-on-one coaching or an audio series.

I regularly run a free event around Australia, "Prosper From Your Passion", and you can sign up by going to; www.authenticeducation.com.au/passion

When you find your message, you find your millions. Financial goals are great to have, and most people initially think it's all about the money. As you progress on your journey, you will discover it's all about who you become in the process of making that money.

I've developed what I like to call the *Prosper From Your Passion Process*. It's basically the three main steps you need to take in order to make money doing what you love.

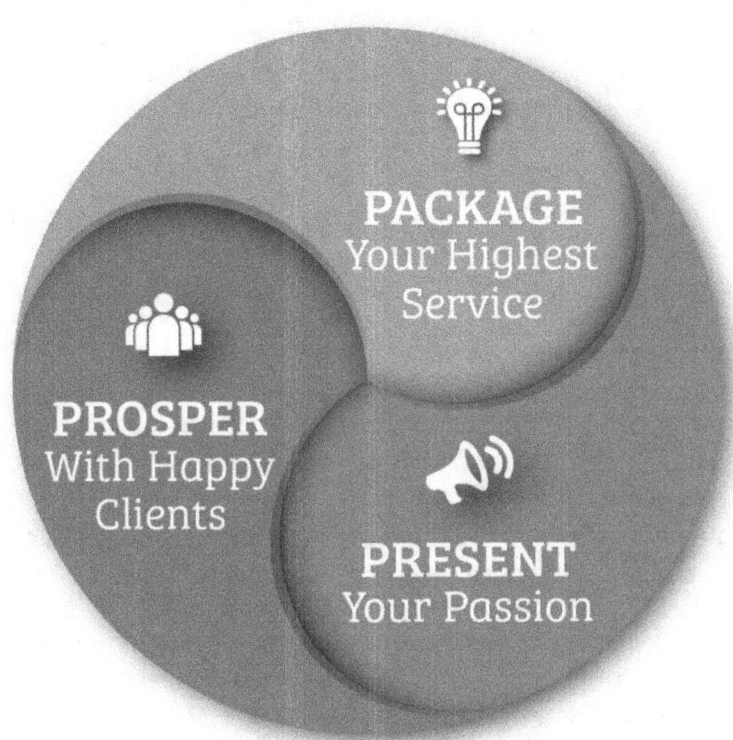

1. **Package Your Highest Service**

Your highest service is what you're most passionate about. It's what you would do even if you didn't get paid. The biggest problem people come up against is that potentially due to a lack of clarity, they never take the time to package up their highest service, so they can share it with the world and make the biggest difference possible.

They lack the clarity to understand what the actual next step is. A lot of people are crystal clear on what they don't like: their job, working nine-five, struggling with their business, having no clients and marketing that's costing them a fortune but gets no return. What's interesting is that they do have clarity about what they want, but sadly because they don't know the next exact steps to take, their brain protects them by preventing them from taking action. This means nobody will get their message, so they can't be of service in the world.

This is exactly why in our "Difference Maker Accelerator" program, we spend six days breaking down the exact steps to knowing what your highest service is and how to go about packaging it for the market.

2. Present Your Passion

Presenting has been the backbone of our success. Being able to craft and deliver public presentations to ever greater numbers of people has meant massive leverage in both sharing a message and growing the business rapidly. This is the reason we encourage our students to present their passion once they've packaged it.

Ninety-five percent or more of the students we're able to serve come from public presentations. This is because public speaking in front of a LIVE audience has so many benefits including:

- being able to build trust with people quickly

- leveraging your time by speaking to large numbers at once

- having their full attention

- gaining immediate feedback from the expressions on their faces while you're presenting

- transferring emotion and inspiring people to take action

- being able to let them experience your style of education firsthand, which is like giving them a test drive of your products and services before they make a decision to buy

I have to say what you will love more than anything else is the feeling you get in your heart knowing you've inspired someone to live an empowered life. There really is nothing quite like it.

How important is it to structure your presentation?

Structure is one of the most critical parts of your presentation. People naturally like to hear stories in certain ways. For instance, having their feelings build, their curiosity awakened and a feeling of inspiration infused into their bodies when they see a presenter sharing their message. People love to gain knowledge and have a good old-fashioned laugh from time to time.

A lot of the people we work with first arrive at our programs wanting to share their message "intuitively" with the world. They have this fantasy that great speakers show up and allow the content to flow through them. The sad truth is, that's not the case. Sure, after years of practice this is possible. However, if you want to make an impact and transform lives, you must first follow a structure.

The most intuitive, inspirational speakers I've observed over the years have all spent hours upon hours practicing within a structure in order to be able to present in a way that moves people into taking action.

There are five core phases a professional speaker must follow if they want to truly turn this art form into a career. They're what we like to call "The Presenter's PRO Formula". At the end of this chapter, you will have the opportunity to download a free copy of an audio program we created that covers in detail each of the phases and exactly how to put together your world class presentation.

Can you please explain the different phases of The Presenter's PRO Formula?

I would love to. Here goes:

Phase 1: Orchestrate Your Outcome

In order to craft a world class presentation, the first question you must ask yourself is this:

At the end of my presentation, what specific action do I want my audience to take?

You must always begin with the end in mind. You would be surprised how many people get this wrong. Before you do anything regarding your presentation, first decide exactly what action you would like your audience to take at the end of your speech.

Here are some examples:

- Commit to meditating daily
- Calling a friend to tell them about the workshop
- Set some goals
- Sign up for a workshop
- Fill in their details for a complimentary coaching session
- Commit to eating vegetables five days a week
- Create a savings plan

From the examples above, let's say your desired action was for the audience to eat more fresh foods. Everything that now goes into the talk is designed to assist your audience members to make that decision and take that action. So as you move into phase two, make sure you continue to ask yourself, *How does this piece of content move them closer to eating more fresh food?*

Remember: The purpose of all education is *new action*, so clarify your action before you do anything else.

Phase 2: Craft Your Presentation

Your presentation will move through three core stages. Understanding each one will allow you to become masterful at creating communication that leaves people on the edge of their seats.

The three stages:

1. Connect

    At the start of your presentation, it's important to connect with every *individual* in the audience through the use of the word YOU. The more you use this word, the more the audience will feel like you're speaking directly to them.

2. Demonstrate

    You need to prove to your audience why they must take new actions relating to the topic you're covering and how this will ultimately solve their current problems.

3. Call to Action

    Ask your audience to take some specific type of action.

Below is a diagram outlining the major content pieces that need to be covered in each of the three stages. Track five of the Presenter's Pro Formula audio program will go into each of the content pieces in far greater detail, so be sure to jump online now and download your own copy at www.authenticeducation.com.au/formula

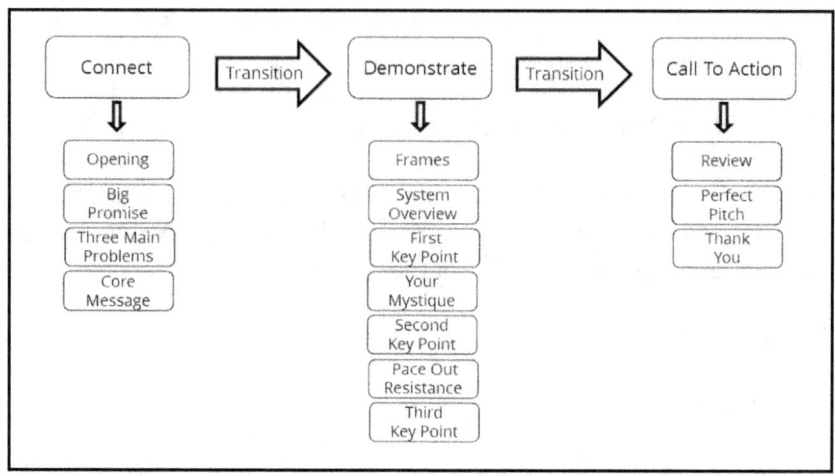

Phase 3: Embody Your Message

As a professional speaker, you need to realise that gone are the days of:

- using a lectern

- having notes

- hiding copious amounts of information in PowerPoint slides

This has been replaced by memory strategies and far more engaging stage presence. Too many people rely on their notes when they should be strengthening their memories. We all have exquisite memories, but it's like a muscle. The more you work it, the stronger it gets.

I learned early on that relying on technology is not always the best technique. If your computer shuts down or the projector stops working, and you haven't bothered to embody your message, then you really are in a tricky situation.

My advice is always to learn how to present with nothing but yourself on stage, and then add the technology as a bonus. Remember: they came to see you speak, to learn something and to be entertained, not watch slides on a screen.

At our program "Present Like a Pro", we teach people three unique memory strategies that allow them to remember and deliver weeks' worth of content without ever having to reference any form of notes. These are some of the methods:

- The photographic memory technique

    This involves putting together a movie of the content you wish to cover and playing the movie in your mind when you get up on stage.

- The pegging technique

    You mentally "peg" content around the room in a specific order.

- The acronym technique.

    This involves breaking down your content into words where each letter stands for a separate point.

You can Google different memory techniques and find the one that most resonates with you. Put your faith in your memory, learn how to harness and master it, and keep training it nonstop. I like to train my memory daily by taking every opportunity possible to remember information rather than writing it down.

Phase 4: Own the Stage

A lot of people think you should master stage work at the beginning, but the truth is you need to master your outcome at the beginning and learn how to craft it correctly. Memorise your message, and then learn how to own the stage.

Owning the stage is about being graceful in your delivery. A dear friend of mine once said to me, "Grace is the removal of all unnecessary movement". I thought that was poetic, and I think about that when I'm training speakers or delivering a presentation.

Sure, you can be taught how and where to stand, as well as the way to use your body to emphasize your points or when speaking about certain topics. However, the first step is to remove all movements that don't serve a purpose. For instance, dancers only perform the precise steps required, and a graceful piece of art only has the precise number of brush strokes. If you remove the unnecessary movements, you can allow your body to naturally flow with how the message wants to come out.

Once this has been achieved, you can learn the finer, more technical aspects of non-verbal communication to enhance your storytelling. These can include:

- body postures, including the Satir categories created by Virginia Satir
- stage anchoring to elicit emotions and time
- mimed models and diagrams

Ray L Birdwhistell published a book entitled *Kinesics and Context*, which is based on his studies of the human body and interpersonal communication. One of his findings was that communication requires the use of all the senses, with words having the smallest percentage of importance in the exchange.

Ray discovered that communication was comprised of these three aspects:

▶ Seven percent words

▶ Thirty-eight percent tonality

▶ Fifty-five percent physiology

So as you can see, it's critically important to be graceful onstage, because ninety-three percent of your message is not what's being said but how it's being conveyed.

At the end of the day the best speakers you will ever see are the ones who are okay with being themselves. The more authentic you can be onstage, the more people will connect with what you have to say. When sharing your message, allow yourself to open your heart and let people in, and you will be sure to make a difference.

Once you've orchestrated your outcome, crafted your presentation, embodied your message and learnt to own the stage, surrender and allow your natural light to shine through your words, and you will captivate hearts and minds around the world.

Phase 5: Manage the Business Model

Some steps that are essential to becoming a professional speaker include:

- knowing how to attract the right people into your community
- being able to fill rooms with an audience that wants to hear your message
- creating desirable packages that solve the problems of audience members
- ensuring you design a solid message to market matches when seeking to build your brand

At the end of the day it's most important for you to remember one fundamental principle about speaking professionally: the same reason they came to see you speak is the exact same reason they will buy.

This is another reason why I like to walk in my audience's shoes before they arrive. If you can focus your presentation on the finer points of exactly why they came to see the presentation, you're sure to connect deeply with everyone in the room. This is such a fundamentally basic concept to understand, yet so easy to miss when you get caught up in the buzz of talking on stage.

Speaking is a lucrative career if you can get the business model correct. I truly believe it's one of the most fulfilling careers upon which you can embark. Every day you get to inspire people to live empowered lives and make a real difference in the world.

I discovered a long time ago that the most fulfilling days are the ones where you solve the most challenging problems in your life and the lives of others. If you get bored with life and are feeling unfulfilled, check in and see how many problems you're solving, as there really is a direct correlation.

What I also discovered was that when you solve problems for others, they often like to show you appreciation in the form of money. The more they appreciate you, the more money they like to give you. The equation is to solve as many problems as you can, and you will be fulfilled and wealthy in every sense. Speaking allows you to solve problems in a leveraged way, due to the number of people you can reach at the same time.

You may be aware that professional speaking is one of the highest paid professions in the world. It's not uncommon for keynote presenters to earn $5,000 for a forty-five minute talk, and professional speakers to make over six figures in a single day. Not a bad way to earn a living when you think about it.

3. Prosper With Happy Clients

This last part of the *Prosper From Your Passion* process is all about inspiring your clients to buy.

I find a lot of clients struggle initially with the sales, until they truly understand that every time they make a sale, they're improving someone's life. In business, selling is about making money, otherwise you don't have a business, and you won't be able to help others by doing what you love. However, I'm not talking about selling to someone who doesn't need what you're offering. Sales should never be about conning someone. It should be based on a genuine desire to help make a difference in a person's life.

These days it's all about educational-based selling. You buy from those who teach the most. Over the years, the word *sales* has taken on such a negative meaning to so many people, that their beliefs stop them from selling their own product or service.

People want to know you genuinely care about them, and this is usually the case. It's the reason why you do what you do and got into business in the first place.

In our "Inspire to Buy" program, we go through a powerful sales process that forever changes the way most people look at sales. We've had students go out and achieve phenomenal sales results after the course, simply based on their enhanced view of the sales process.

Do you have any new products or services on the horizon?

A recent survey we ran found that Australians would sacrifice up to $10,000 of their annual salary to feel happier at work, and this is something we're actively addressing with our entire suite of educational products and services.

 We'll be launching two brand-new live events that cover mindset and self-empowerment strategies, with a strong focus on how to coach yourself through life's challenges. They will be free to attend.

We also have a range of innovative new products coming out, which cover our patented coaching methodologies for life and business. On top of that, we're offering a number of online programs that will cover everything from digital marketing to how to write bestselling books.

These will all dovetail nicely with our signature offering, PHD. It stands for Programs for Heart-Centred Difference-Markers. The PHD program is five core programs that help people address the key issues they need to solve if they want to succeed in a business that helps others improve the quality of their lives.

1. Productivity and systems

2. Mindset

3. Packaging and marketing (end-to-end business lifecycle)

4. Presenting from the stage

5. Education based selling

To top it all off, we're pleased to announce that we'll be running an event specifically designed for teenagers. They acquire the tools necessary to ensure they leave school and find a career that's both challenging and fulfilling, so it's in alignment with what they're most passionate about.

Parents have been asking us for an event like this for over six years, and we're finally in a position that allows us to give back. The event will be completely free for teenagers to attend, and we plan on keeping it free forever.

How do you fund these new online products?

Through many painful lessons in business, Cham and I have managed to learn that looking after the cash flow, being wise with spending and keeping a *cash cushion*, allows us to capitalise on opportunities as they arise and maintain the success of any new growth venture. Therefore, all of our new ventures are funded internally by the business.

Authentic Education has never taken a bank loan, nor has it had any investors come on board along the way. When we began, Cham and I put in a total $5,000 each to buy a projector, a microphone, some speakers, a few banners and some other little knick-knacks, and we were off and racing.

This financial position allows us to have complete freedom in our creativity and business direction without any fear of failure, because we have the financial strength to constantly trial new ideas.

What is one technique to practice if you want more success?

Over the years I've tried everything from hypnosis, to crystal healing, to sage smudging, to visualization.

In the end, the most powerful process I've done and practice regularly is list writing. This requires nothing more than a paper and pen and writing down all of the reasons you deserve success. I usually suggest you write down 100-200 reasons nonstop, and just let then flow from inside of you.

Start with this exercise:

Write down twenty reasons why you deserve to earn money from what you're passionate about: Some examples are below to get you started. Just begin writing down whatever comes into your mind.

- Because I'm funny
- Because I finished school
- Because I'm a nice person

- Because I'm dedicated

- Because I work hard

Keep going until you have two-hundred reasons. You can do this for any topic in which you'd like to become successful.

What this process does is to fire and wire your neurons (thinking cells). It's all about changing your beliefs at a subconscious level, because if you don't believe you deserve it, you won't achieve the success you deserve.

And lastly...practice authentic appreciation. There are a lot of people who talk about the concept of having an *attitude of gratitude*, which sounds really good in theory, and it even rhymes, which makes it significantly more appealing.

The only problem with this principle is that people often struggle with being able to feel gratitude on cue. Think about this for a second. If I were to ask you to feel gratitude right now, what actions would you take?

Gratitude and appreciation are virtually the exact same feeling. However, appreciation is far easier to bring into the body. If I asked you to bring to mind something you appreciate, you would be able to easily think of something, which would cause you to instantly feel the feeling in your body.

"So how do I practice authentic appreciation?" I hear you ask.

Well it's simple. Set aside a maximum of five minutes per day. During that time, gently close your eyes and imagine some of what you appreciate in life. These can be anything. Here are some examples:

- A walk along the beach
- A conversation with a dear friend
- Learning something new
- A specific achievement
- A comfortable bed
- Having fun playing games
- Having time to meditate

As you bring these into your imagination, allow yourself to surrender into that subtle sensation of appreciation.

The reason why it's so important to do is because of what scientists call *cognitive bias*. As you spend time daily reflecting on what you appreciate, you create a new set of rules in your mind, as well as a new set of biases. Once these biases are set up, you filter the external world in accordance with them. What this means in real terms is that you begin to unconsciously sort for what to appreciate and therefore end up discovering more to be grateful for.

The saying in the industry is, "What you focus on, expands", which is a simplified way of explaining cognitive bias. Keep in mind that the more you appreciate in your life, the more you get to appreciate. Oh, and by the way, it feels really good, so that should be reason enough to try it out for a few days at the very least.

Remember, **life rewards action,** so go out there and get started today making a difference and a living doing what you love.

Benjamin J Harvey

 To discover more about how Ben can help you *Elevate Your Success*, visit

www.elevate-books.com/success

Anna Hartmann

Bearfoot Business

Anna Hartmann is the owner and founder of Bearfoot Wholefoods on the Gold Coast and is the single mother to two daughters.

Anna was juggling an online degree, a part-time night shift job, intense Crossfit training and sole parenting, when a bad case of pneumonia brought training to a grinding halt. After taking a closer look at her own nutritional health, as well as what she was putting in her children's lunchboxes, she decided to defer her studies and see where her little hobby paleo business would take her.

The result of all of Anna's hard work is that Bearfoot Wholefoods has evolved into a full-scale manufacturing operation, shipping around 1.2tn of product around Australia each month, and will soon export overseas. Anna feels her personal experiences put her in a good position to promote a healthy lifestyle to others. Her life purpose is to inspire people to be the best version of themselves.

Anna Hartmann
Bearfoot Business

What's the worst thing that's ever happened to you, and how did you overcome it?

It happened on New Year's Eve in 2009. I was thirty-five years old with two young daughters under the age of six. After many years of enduring my husband's agonizing cycles of depression, anxiety and anger, I was exhausted emotionally, mentally and spiritually. My husband had recently become unemployed *again*, and I was waitressing split shifts to make ends meet. I didn't know what day it was, and I was tired all of the time, but I did know one thing: I finally had the courage to leave my ten-year-long abusive marriage. I could see the future impact of our home environment on our children, and it was my duty to not have them grow up believing that living in anger and negativity is normal.

I didn't acknowledge my husband's long history of mental health issues until midway into our relationship, and I didn't accept I was in an abusive relationship until nearly six years *after* I left. He had little contact with his children, despite my tireless efforts to remain amicable, which was fear-based and guilt-driven, and encouraged him to be a responsible, involved parent. His diagnosis of post-traumatic stress disorder, or PTSD, totally consumed him, and he simply couldn't find a way to fulfil his parental obligations.

He then moved in with a new girlfriend and her children in early 2015. In June he came to visit and wanted to discuss taking the children on a more regular basis. After five and a half years of single parenting in the literal sense of the word, and with no child support, I was certainly prepared to embrace this step forward for him. I did, however, want to know he could meet his financial responsibilities as a parent and provide an emotionally stable environment for his children. Two years prior, our eldest daughter, age nine at the time, spent over a year in therapy for anxiety after she experienced bullying at school. He'd told her, "The world's not a very nice place. There aren't many nice people, and you just have to deal with it." I had to learn a whole new skill set to help manage her anxiety, which is still a daily task, especially given her recent diagnosis of Aspergers.

When I asked how he was financially and emotionally, what followed propelled me back to our marriage, but for the first time I acknowledged the domestic violence, and our children were fully exposed to it. This left me to pick up the pieces for months afterwards. Then to add insult to injury, a judge decided in his favour, which proved to him that he never committed domestic violence.

In the midst of all of this, I was on my own personal quest to find more compassion and forgiveness that went far beyond my ex-husband's behaviour. An internal battle raged inside of me, until I understood that compassion and forgiveness are not signs of weakness. I discovered I could forgive him but that I also couldn't control anyone else's thoughts, words and actions. Recognising I needed extra help to stand up for myself, I applied for a protection order and am still navigating the court system at the time of this writing. It's confusing to my ex-husband, because for so long I allowed him to treat me as he wanted. He continues to fight the world by fighting me.

At the same time, in June of 2015, two Gold Coast women and a six-year-old little girl from Brisbane tragically lost their lives in domestic violence incidents, which sparked a nationwide campaign and review of our domestic violence laws. One of those women was my beautician's sister, and in January of 2016 I attended the inaugural event, A Day for Nadia, to celebrate her life and to encourage communities everywhere to start talking about their experiences in order to bring domestic violence out of the shadows and into the light.

Anna Hartmann

Has there been a situation when you met adversity and had to use your wits to get yourself out of it?

I was twenty years old and headed to Airlie Beach on a bus with all of my belongings, including my antique silver saxophone my grandfather had given me. The plan was to find hospitality work on the Whitsunday islands, so I could live the dream. My point of contact was a step cousin, and after two weeks of him harassing me, my dream was over. I made the decision to go home to the Gold Coast.

Luck would have it that I was able to hitch a ride on a small sailing yacht with another girl I met in Airlie. It was, and still is, common for sailors to advertise for crew, and many backpackers take up this offer to add sailing to their holiday experiences. So away we went, learning how to tie knots, take the helm (steer), and read the charts. The trip would take roughly four weeks, and we were pretty excited about the whole thing.

About a week and a half in, my experience wasn't exciting anymore. The skipper was volatile, aggressive and had stolen property. My friend and I didn't feel comfortable and wanted to flee, but it's a bit hard when you're at sea and can't even see land. We were coming up to the semi-inhabited Percy Island that was famous among sailors for its massive timber A-frame on the beach where people would leave a piece of sailing memorabilia for all eternity. As we pulled in to anchor, the skipper started abusing us, because we couldn't anchor *his* boat properly. My friend had only minimal experience on boats, and I had none.

We went ashore, where I took my friend for a walk and a serious chat. I knew it wasn't safe for us to get back on that boat. She was worried about being stranded, but I stood firm, even though I had no idea what I was going to do. I just trusted my intuition to guide me. I told her I wasn't getting back on that boat, even if she did.

That same night we met Brett and Gary, who were also sailing down from Airlie Beach, and we chatted for a bit. I wasn't pitching to them to rescue us, but I told them about our situation, and rescue us they did. After two glorious weeks of sailing, they delivered us safely back to Mooloolaba, Queensland. Twenty-one years later, Brett and Gary remain two of my closest friends, and I met them at a time when potentially everything could have turned out differently.

What's the best thing that's ever happened to you?

I'm passionate about health and wellbeing from a three-dimensional perspective: nutritional, physical and emotional. In the past, my experiences in life have led me to address only one or two of these at the same time. I tended to ignore my own emotional health, which eventually manifested in a variety of "unexplained" illnesses.

When a twenty-three year old turns up at the GP with Bell's palsy for no valid reason, the medical world is a little baffled. It wasn't until quite a few years later when I ended up in hospital with pneumonia, also with no warning signs and at the fittest I'd ever been in my life, that I started to investigate the effects of stress on my physical body.

With the help of my sister, clinical and health psychologist Dr Peta Stapleton, who's also Associate Professor at Bond University, I recognized a pattern in my life where "regular" types of illnesses would severely affect me. Like for instance a fever associated with a common cold would be so high, I would hallucinate. I remember as a young child my mother putting me in lukewarm vinegar baths and shortening the timeframe in which she administered paracetamol (acetaminophen), to try and bring my fever down.

Peta is also one of Australia's leading experts and trainers in the energy therapy technique of EFT, which is the Emotional Freedom Technique, commonly known as tapping. The method utilizes some of the ancient Chinese acupressure points that are tapped while you focus on a problem or issue. The combination of these somatic and cognitive elements, or tapping, quiets down the amygdala, the stress response part of the brain, so you can become calmer and think more clearly about the problem. The power of EFT is that it helps to identify the origin of your patterns when limiting beliefs were formed and then releases them.

With the success of Peta's clinical research, it's now scientifically proven to work in the area of obesity and weight management. In 2014 I attended Peta's EFT tapping workshops regarding food cravings, pain and money. At this point, my life started to change significantly, and in 2015 I completed EFT training.

There's no shortage of advice that we should eat healthy and exercise, but for many people it's virtually impossible to change old habits from a conscious level. I have a technique I can share with people that will not only address food cravings but empower them to change all aspects of their life. I now understand how connected we really are. I highly recommend joining the priority list of an event coming up at Bond University on the Gold Coast in 2017, called Mind Heart Connect. Go to www.mindheartconnect.com. It's a transformational forum bringing together experts in evidence-based practices inspiring wellness and resiliency.

You can find out more about Peta Stapleton at www.petastapleton.com.

What's the one message you wish to share with the world?

Every person on this planet is destined for greatness. If you break it down, all you need to claim your birthright is be kind to yourself. This means putting yourself first and being brave in the face of adversity, hardship and challenge and having the courage to stand up for what you believe is right.

What do you think is your life purpose?

My life purpose is to inspire others to become the best version of themselves by focusing their energy on their health and wellbeing. I do this through my attitude, actions and service. I share my story of hardship and triumph to give others hope that they can also change their future and to look inside of themselves to find the answers.

When I look back at all of the times I was sick, I can see there was always an emotional aspect I was failing to address. It would eventually show up physically, because it still needed to be processed. Through my experiences, if I can help others see the importance of a holistic approach to their health and life, I'm more than living out my purpose.

It's been said many ways, but this is my favourite:

> "There is nothing outside of yourself that can ever enable you to get better, stronger, richer, quicker, or smarter. Everything is within. Everything exists. Seek nothing outside of yourself."
> ~ Miyamoto Musashi, The Book of Five Rings

What do you believe you've been put on the planet to do?

I believe we're all on this planet to serve. This quote by His Holiness, the fourteenth Dalai Lama, hangs in my kitchen:

The True Meaning of Life

"We are visitors on this planet. We are here for ninety or one hundred years at the very most. During that period we must try to do something good, something useful, with our lives. If you can contribute to other people's happiness, you will find the true goal, the true meaning of life."

I didn't always understand this. I was brought up to believe I had to get a good education and be a good person. In my early twenties I began searching for meaning and purpose by reading books like *The Way of the Peaceful Warrior* by Dan Millman, *The Celestine Prophecy* by James Redfield and *The Tao Te Ching* by Lao Tzu.

Only now do I truly understand the relationship between serving others and my happiness, peace and prosperity. Even after I started my business, I questioned my purpose. I kept thinking, *Am I doing what I'm meant to be doing?* Rather than searching again for meaning and purpose, I began to invest in myself, because I realized that in order to serve others I first needed to value myself. I have to be the best version of me, which is a lifelong pursuit of self-development and improvement.

I've always believed that when the student is ready, the teacher appears. My teachers over the last few years have come from books like *The Monk Who Sold His Ferrari* by Robin Sharma, *Zero Limits* by Dr Joe Vitale & Dr Ihaleakala Hew Len and *The Impersonal Life* by Joseph Benner, which was recommended via a Wayne Dyer video after his passing. The message is the same in all of these texts, which is that you need to serve. I saw Oprah in Brisbane in December of 2015, and her message was the same.

If you were speaking to your younger self, what advice would you give?

First of all, you're never alone in this universe. When the going gets tough, search deep within and find the strength that's always been waiting there for you. Know that if you seek answers, you already have them. All you have to do is ask. Become best friends with yourself, and learn to trust your own judgment.

You have the potential to become your own worst enemy or master of your destiny. There are going to be many people who will consciously and unconsciously try to steer you away from your dreams. Act graciously, but only listen to the voice deep inside of you. Set ridiculous, unrealistic goals while focussing only on the end result with an unwavering resolve. When you fall short of those goals, celebrate all of the achievements along the way. As you look back, you will see how far you've come and how far behind everyone is who only set realistic goals.

Embrace every challenge as the opportunity you need to grow. Everything is perfect as it is, and everyone is at the perfect point they need to be, including you. Understand you can't control another human being's thoughts or actions, but you can control your own. Practicing gratitude is easy. It's the golden key. Forgiveness will set you free but will take longer to master. Spend time on your own every day. Above all, you only ever have to work on yourself. Look into the mirror and learn to love everything that looks back at you.

How would you like to be remembered?

As an inspiration to women and single mothers everywhere. I want to be proof that no matter what happens, every woman has what it takes within them to walk a new path and create absolutely anything.

What do you think people's biggest issues are?

I think one of the biggest issues people face is the feeling of worthiness. In other words, valuing themselves, which is related to a theme of *I'm not good enough*. As Dr John Demartini teaches, people subordinate by putting others' values before their own and then allow their days to fill up with low-priority tasks as opposed to high-priority ones.

What's the best way to help people deal with these issues?

Education and application. Benjamin J Harvey has built an entire business educating people on how to achieve success in all areas of life and to live authentically doing what they love. The practical application of his course material guarantees success. I've personally met Ben a number of times, and I highly recommend his training to anyone seeking to make a difference in the world. Ben is an expert on values. He guides people to identify what their set of values are and how to fulfil them from a place of self-love. Ben goes into a full-depth analysis of this in his chapter titled "Shadow Values" from the Millionaire Motivators book *How to Find What You Love to Do and Get Paid to Do It!*

Based on your experience, what's the best tip you could give?

Put yourself first. I don't mean in a selfish way but certainly in a non-negotiable one. Women are taught from a young age to put everyone else first. There's a real danger that when we get to be middle-aged, we're worn out, bitter and resentful, with nothing left to give and more than likely a burning desire to still make a difference somehow.

In order to truly help others, you need to be the best version of yourself, and that means putting yourself first. My beautician, the one who lost her sister to domestic violence, launched a new program called "Best Love Affair". It's all about indulging in quality time with yourself by taking responsibility for filling your own love tank, like making yourself a special breakfast or having a bubble bath at six am.

What's the biggest mistake people make in the area of starting their own business?

I think people make two mistakes:

1. Thinking every single detail needs to be perfect before starting.

2. Listening to everyone else's advice about how they should run their business.

How did you become interested in the importance of whole foods combined with a balanced lifestyle?

When I left my marriage in 2009, I joined Crossfit Gold Coast to become a fit and healthy single parent. The fittest crew in this gym advocated food plans like the Zone Diet and the Paleo Diet for peak performance and lean muscle. Eighteen months later, at the fittest point in my life due to my physical training, I was struck down with pneumonia. I thought it was from regular lapses in my diet, so I started looking not only at my own health and nutrition but also at what I was putting in my children's lunch boxes, which was highly processed packaged foods deemed "school canteen approved". I was fit in the context of the amount of training I was doing, but my nutrition was not a hundred percent.

This is when I started my business, Anna's Gourmet Paleo, in 2012. During the first year I lacked a whole lot of physical activity and emotional health, so it's no surprise I went searching for balance in the second and third years. My own personal experience now puts me in a good position to promote a healthy lifestyle to others.

How do you go from a concept or idea to a business?

Luca, my business partner, and I sat around for a year or so talking about a food product idea, along with my ex-husband, during a more amicable time. Clearly the universe had other plans, because as I listened to them discussing how the name, logo design and labels had to be perfect before starting, I jumped online to do some research on homemade paleo food. I played around in the kitchen with a couple of recipes, more interested in how the product tasted if/when accepted in the marketplace, and how it could be produced in volume without compromising its integrity. Yes, part of me was future projecting, but a bigger part of me was simply taking initiative.

Luca was training at a Crossfit gym, and some of my friends from my Crossfit days had branched out and opened their own gyms. We gave them some samples of our paleo granola, and they wanted to sell it. That's when I thought, *Ok, we need a name, logo and packaging*. Those early days of the "hobby" business had me using basic computer skills to create an even more basic sticker we printed ourselves on black and white label paper. Stores like Mrs Flannery's came on board and supported us with those home-printed labels. It proved we had a great product, and we just needed to improve in the area of retail branding. My brother's graphic design skills are responsible for the first two phases of our logo design, which carried us through the first three years of business, until we were in a financial position to rebrand on a more commercial level.

Many years earlier I'd gained experience in office management and accounts payable/receivable, so I was able to apply these skills to build the administration side of the business. If you don't have these skills, a great place to start is in your computer Office program where you can search hundreds of templates to create basic sales invoices. Also, search your state government business website for more information on the requirements for business setup and structure, registration, whether you need your own ABN or to register for GST. It's all there, including contact details if you want to speak to a real person.

What's your most inspiring story?

One of my first customers was a bulk foods store in Burleigh Heads on the Gold Coast. It's called Helen's Heavenly Bulk Foods. As our granola is sold from a bulk bin, it's perfectly normal that a customer would get home and not remember the product manufacturer's details displayed on the in-store bin.

In November of 2013 I received an email from Nat Medhurst, an Australian Netballer, via my online store contact form. She said she'd bought our granola from the Burleigh store and wanted to give me some feedback but couldn't remember where the product came from. At the time she was living in Brisbane playing for the Brisbane Firebirds, as well as the Australian team. She'd found a packaged version of our granola at one of our Brisbane retailers with our details and asked if we had any stockists in Western Australia (WA), as she was about to relocate to play for the Perth Wildcats.

I was over the moon with her email. I could have simply replied that we didn't have any stockists in WA, and she could order online. But for me, action speaks louder than words. I emailed Nat back and asked if she'd like to meet with me to discuss the possibility of a product sponsorship agreement. Did I have any experience in this area? NO! Was I nervous about meeting Nat Medhurst, one of Australia's elite athletes and talking about little ol' me and my hobby business? *Hell, yes*!

The meeting went well, and we sponsored Nat throughout 2014 and 2015. She posted photos on social media each month of the creative things she'd done with our products, and we teamed up for promotional competitions. In 2014, Nat wound up winning the gold with the Australian team at the Commonwealth Games in Glasgow.

Since that first email from Nat, we've gone on to sponsor other athletes from the International Mixed Martial Arts (MMA) arena, namely Laurence Griffiths, a paleo advocate from the United Kingdom. You can go to http://www.effectivehealthandfitness.com, to find out more. In recent times, we've teamed with Nobel Lee, who represents Busiido BJJ from Brunei and is on Instagram as *nobelee*.

When opportunity knocks, sometimes you only have a small window in which to act. If you show courage, the rewards are waiting for you on the other side. The universe is constantly offering up opportunity. Will you notice?

What courses have you taken that enabled you to start or build your business?

About three months into the business, I completed a diploma for small business management. It taught me the administration skills I already knew, plus everything else I needed. I learned how to do a business plan, which is important if your business is growing like wildfire, and you need to become friends with your bank manager.

I was still a sole trader a year into the business, when Luca and I enrolled in a series of courses with Benjamin J Harvey and Authentic Education in Sydney. At the first course we met Giorgio Genaus, a coach trained in the Demartini method, and I invested in a three-month coaching program with him via Skype. Giorgio taught me the true value of the concept. *There's two sides to everything.* Now if ever I perceive a person or event as "bad" or "terrible" I stop myself and ask, *What's the upside, and how does this benefit me?*, because you can't have one without the other. That's what balance is. All of my life I was so consumed with being super-duper positive and optimistic, I kept attracting the polar opposite to balance me, which was super-duper negativity.

All of the men in my life had a victim mentality and massive insecurities. I've had friends and staff members who create drama and manifest hostility in their lives. Since I've applied Demartini's method, these experiences are few and far between. I accept I have all of the emotions inside of me, and I adopt a more neutral awareness instead of trying to be over-the-top positive to avoid negativity.

What's the best way people can achieve a good life-work balance?

Learn the importance of prioritising. If you don't set high-priority daily, weekly and monthly tasks, your days will fill up with low-priority tasks. Yes, you'll be busy, but you won't achieve anything meaningful.

Again, this is where putting yourself first comes in. Separate and schedule your work, family and *me* time. Have your non-negotiable time slots, and summon the strength to say no when someone tries to steal them.

Oprah talked about this in December of 2015 when I had the privilege of attending the "An Evening with Oprah" event. The message is that you may think if you say yes to everybody, they will like you and think you're nice, but there are more important qualities to possess than being nice. For instance, worthiness. If you don't value your own time, how can you expect anyone else to? The more you say yes to others, the less you say yes to yourself, your family, your dreams and your balance.

What are your tips for getting through a difficult time in life?

There's no challenge without reward. Embrace the hardship, because it's the only way growth happens. Know that it will pass, and it doesn't define who you are. Seek out support from friends, family, books, mentors or an expert who can guide you through processing the emotions. Honour the process itself.

Why are goals important?

If you want to improve any aspect of your life like money, health or relationships, you can't just make a wish, sit back and hope for the best. It's good to realise the importance of goal setting and how it can change your life dramatically when you put some effort into it. Nothing great was ever achieved without setting goals and consistently working towards them. Aim for the moon, and you might just reach the stars.

What's the best way to set and achieve goals?

I learned this formula using EFT, and it has worked best for me.

- Write down your goal. Include the date and as much detail as possible, as if it's already happened. For instance, *It's July 10, 2017, and I've just picked up my brand-new blue diesel automatic Subaru Outback. I feel amazing!*

- Read your goal out aloud, and listen for the doubtful voice in your head. In EFT we call them tail-enders, and they're the sentences that sound something like this: *But I've never owned a new car before* or *How is that ever going to happen?* or *I can't do that, and I definitely don't feel amazing.*

- Use the EFT tapping technique to reduce all of the doubt associated with the goal. This essentially targets any limiting beliefs and conditioning around the area of success.

I also use vision boards, and the kids really love getting involved. Say we want to go on our first overseas skiing holiday. We get a big piece of cardboard and stick magazine clippings all over it of everything to do with a skiing holiday. We write in big colourful pens where we're going, the date, and most importantly, how we *feel* when we're there. We place the vision board where we spend a lot of time and build excitement around it. Pam Grout, author of *E-Squared* and *E-Cubed* explains how the energetic field of the universe works. Since you're an energetic being, you can trick the universe into manifesting what you want just by focussing most of your energy on the feelings associated with your goals.

I'd never bought a brand-new car until January, 2016. A few years ago I was the one thinking, *How could I ever do that?* But in just a few short years, everything I've done regarding goal setting has impacted my life far beyond anything I could have wished for.

What mindset do you believe is needed to create a great life?

You need a growth and abundant mindset. I've used meditation and hypnosis audio to help me, and I truly believe this has been a major factor in how my life has transformed over the last few years. Not only is my food business expanding, other opportunities are opening up that have nothing to do with it but will serve to grow my business even more and help shape me into my future self.

How do you start your day?

Right when I get up in the morning, I make my bed. My parents met in the Royal Australian Air Force (RAAF), and I believe there's definitely a place for the disciplinary mindset.

I'm nearly always up before anybody else in the house. After I've made my bed I prepare a cup of tea, sit out back, and come rain, hail or shine, I project love out into the universe. Then I write in my gratitude journal a minimum of five things I'm grateful for.

Does visualisation work?

Absolutely! In his book *The Monk Who Sold His Ferrari*, Robin Sharma offers many practical tools you can apply for health, wealth and happiness. One I've adopted is a simple mantra I repeat mentally thirty times a day. It can be done on its own for general success, but if you add visualisation of your goals, the results are profound. The mantra itself is:

I am more than I appear to be, all the world's strength and power resides in me.

Beware: this visualization works just as well if you're focusing on the negative.

Name one thing someone could do now to change their life.

Read *The Richest Man in Babylon* by George Clason, and start with the first step, which is the ten-percent rule. Whatever you earn, one tenth is yours to keep. When the universe sees you increasingly valuing yourself, it will present more opportunities for you to continue this theme.

Was there one thing that when you got it, everything else seemed to fall into place?

Gratitude. Early in 2015 I discovered *Ho'oponopono*, the ancient Hawaiian problem-solving method. It's a deeply spiritual, yet non-religious practice, which at a basic level involves love, gratitude, repentance and forgiveness. At a deeper level, this practice will challenge the core of your very soul. After a few months of practice and teaching my children the concept, we all attended a weekend workshop, where my daughters kept themselves occupied with lots of artwork. At the break on the second day, my eldest daughter, who was eleven at the time, went up to the presenter and advised her that lots of the adults were asking the same thing over and over and again, and they just weren't getting it!

The way I practice gratitude is writing in my gratitude journal a simple list of five things I'm grateful for. Now it's all falling into place every day.

To discover more about how Anna can help you *Elevate Your Success*, visit

www.elevate-books.com/success

Shandra Moran

CEO You

Shandra's broad experience and training includes over ten years in the media industry. She's an award-winning radio promotions and marketing director, values-based professional coach, mentor and internationally accredited money breakthrough coach.

An early midlife crisis led Shandra to leave the media industry and follow her passion for people development. After training as a coach, she held a senior management role within a learning and development company.

Following a diagnosis of severe adrenal fatigue in 2014, Shandra reinvented her professional life once again when she left to create The Transit Lounge, a boutique coaching consultancy devoted to helping women improve their relationship and results with money, so they can be well paid doing what they love.

Shandra Moran
CEO You

How did you become interested in the concept of being the CEO of Brand You?

I think I first became interested in the concept of personal branding when I was program director of Nova 937 in Perth. A big part of that role was managing the on air-talent. I'd wind up talking to many of them about this concept, particularly when it came to clients wanting to do sponsorships or brand endorsements. Either there was a natural fit between products and people or there wasn't.

These conversations extended into the off air-team I managed. For them it was more about how they collaborated and worked together and who came to mind when promotion opportunities came up. For instance, who would or wouldn't be right for the role or first thoughts when receiving a call about a reference check.

The concept of instant associations really struck a chord with me. When it came time to make a decision about re-signing my contract at Nova or leaving to do something new, I didn't realise at the time it was a point of brand review for me and reassessing where I was, where and who I wanted to be and what I'd have to do to get there.

The concept of being the CEO of my own brand has stayed with me ever since and has informed a great deal of the work I've done on myself and with my clients.

What's been your biggest life lesson?

There have been many.

One that comes to mind is to trust myself more and become friends with feeling a little bit uncomfortable. It sounds weird, and maybe it is, but at the same time it's an incredibly powerful concept. If you only do certain activities because they're familiar and comfortable, then essentially you've stopped growing and going outside of your comfort zone. The more you can get used to the discomfort of unfamiliarity, the greater your growth path and positive results will be.

The discomfort is a feedback mechanism, and your response can either take you down the path of growth or to a dead end. I'm not sure if you can ever get comfortable with feeling uncomfortable, but if you're able to just become friends with it, you'll likely be surprised by the new opportunities that come your way.

What's the one message you wish to share with the world?

You're a brand, just like Apple, Nike and Virgin. You're the CEO of Brand You. Your brand is not about being famous. It has to do with how others would describe you to someone who hasn't met you, what they think you're capable of and what they would recommend you for. It's the unique combination of your strengths, passions, experience and attributes. Who and what shows up when you enter the room or work on a project. Of all the projects you develop, none of them will be as important as the growth and wellbeing of your own brand.

You're not just the CEO of Brand You. You're also the marketing manager and the head of finance, operations, HR, innovation and quality control, so it's a big job. You need to invest the same amount of passion, time, and energy into developing your skills as you would in any other role. If you don't reflect on, discover, define and develop Brand You, then you may never reach your potential.

In my time working in radio and beyond, I've come across many people who have an inaccurate opinion of themselves, because they're unaware how they're coming across. I remember a conversation I had with an announcer who I often got complaints about from people on the team. He thought he was being passionate, committed and confident. Others predominantly experienced him as aggressive, rude and arrogant.

When I shared this feedback with him, he was genuinely devastated. It hadn't been his intention to come across that way, but his communication style was terrible. He had to reflect on who he wanted to be and what he wanted to be known for, so he could create a way of behaving that built the brand he wanted.

The starting point of building your brand is to clarify what the business of your life is all about. What do you want to be, do and have, now and in the future?

You then build your brand through:

- mindfulness : how present and self-aware you are

- money: how you create and spend it

- meaningful work: the value you provide to others through the work you do.

What's the best thing that's ever happened to you and why?

It's interesting, because I've had some really fantastic events happen in my life so far, and I plan to have many more. Other than meeting and marrying my awesome husband, I think it's being diagnosed with severe adrenal fatigue in July of 2014, because my adrenal glands were struggling to function normally as a result of overwork and stress. Some people think it's a bit odd I would think of that as the best thing to happen, but it gave me permission to accept I wasn't just being lazy. It was tangible feedback from my body that it was exhausted. Literally, completely exhausted. What's fantastic is that it wasn't worse.

It wasn't chronic fatigue…yet. It wasn't cancer. I had a choice to do something about it. I remember my beautiful naturopath, Emma, saying to me, "This has been a long time coming. It's not just a year of working too much. It's due to years and years of overworking." She also told me it was going to take a long time to heal and that nothing heals like joy. I cried, because I realised it had been quite a long time since joy was a regular part of my work life. She'd asked me about my hobbies, and I laughed and thought, *Who has time for hobbies???*

In the subsequent weeks, Mick and I went to Bali for a circuit-breaker trip, where I created a five point wellness plan with a bonus sixth point. When I went back to see Emma, I told her about my plan with the bonus point, and she laughed about my over-achieving ways.

Anyway, the diagnosis led me to what I call *Shut up, think and feel time*. I reflected on where I was, what I was doing and how aligned I felt in utilising my passions, strengths and values in my occupation. I'd loved my job for years, and although I worked long hours in a fairly stressful role, I'd experienced a great sense of fulfilment and connection with my co-workers.

When the situation started to change, and my role shifted more and more away from my true strengths, I believe my body started sending me signals that it was time for me to move on to something else, but I ignored them for quite a long time.

What is a big life issue people seem to have?

Playing it safe. They worry about what others think or feel, like if they don't have the full picture, they won't take the first step. So many people are stuck in a job or situation they're unhappy with. . They complain about their *woe is me* champagne problem but don't actually do anything about it.

There's so much choice in almost every situation. If you don't like something, change it. You may not be able to have it exactly the way you want it right away, and that's fine. Your life is your life's work, so you don't want it to be done before lunchtime tomorrow. Most people take themselves way too seriously. I've been guilty of this in the past, and it's exhausting. Now I'm always trying to find ways to be true to myself and take everything more lightly.

With all of your experience, what's the biggest tip you could give to people?

One of my past coaches, Vashti, helped me remember to *Be Here Now*.

I think it's important to realise you're given one mad, crazy, amazing life, and your purpose is to live it to the fullest of your potential. Experience it and create it to be as beautiful and inspiring to yourself and others as you possibly can.

I remember at the peak of my radio career, when ratings results were fantastic and I had all of the hallmarks of success, I asked myself, *Is this it?* I enjoyed it, and it was often a lot of fun, but I wanted something more.

When I resigned from my role as program director of Nova 937, my boss said to me, "But what will you *do*?" Bless him. He thought he was trying to convince me to stay, but he didn't realise how that statement helped convince me to leave.

I knew there was more I could do. I had no idea what exactly, but I backed myself enough that given time and space, I would figure it out. Waiting for someone, or something, else to make me happy, give me the answer, or give me permission, was never going to happen. I had to go out and find my own way.

So my tip is to back yourself. Do whatever it takes to get to know who you really are, and then consistently take action to be that person.

Bring that brand to life. The world is waiting for you.

What's the biggest mistake people make in the area of being Brand You?

Thinking that branding has to do with becoming someone else. When I first started talking about personal branding, most people thought I was a stylist and that their brand was, for example, being the person who always wore red. That's so not it at all.

Yes, personal appearance is one aspect of your brand. However, it's only one small part, and it's informed by the foundation of your brand. Have you ever met someone who presented well in terms of talking the talk or how they dressed or the car they drove, but when it came time for them to take action, it turned out they had no follow through?

Also, there are people who try to manufacture a brand for their professional life that's completely different from their personal one, as if it's a mask they wear when they're working. That's a recipe for disaster. For example, people in the health profession who smoke or have other bad habits that aren't aligned with the message they give their clients. The days of this method working well are OVER. Social media, and the interconnectedness of the world, means you're always on show.

It's exhausting trying to be someone you're not, so it's a far better strategy to be genuine and build your brand around that. Don't think it only matters how you act in front of important people, because you know what? They're all important people.

Anyone you meet in any context could be a potential client, new boss, referral partner, joint venture opportunity, journo, or someone with a massive Instagram following. You just never know. If you're always genuinely you, and you're clear and aligned to your brand, then you never have to worry about being on show or found out.

Do you have an approach to becoming the CEO of Brand You?

As the CEO of brand you, you're responsible for the wellbeing and sustainability of the business of your life. The definition of wellbeing is the contented state of feeling happy, healthy and prosperous, and I believe the best way to build your Brand You mindset is by cultivating health through *mindfulness*, happiness by doing *meaningful work* you love and prosperity by developing positive results with *money*.

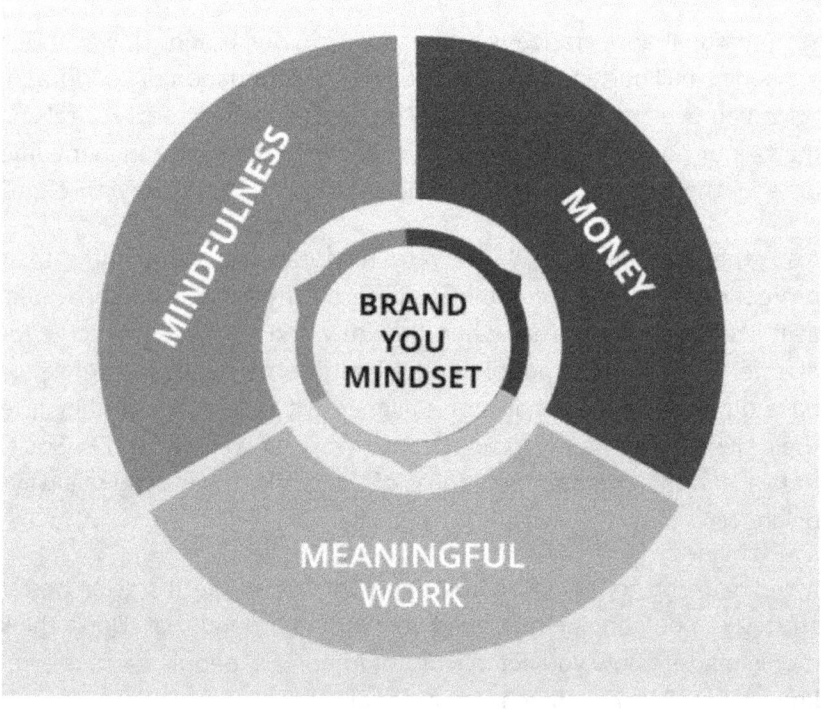

How did you decide on the name and logo for your business?

When I left my last corporate role, I'd been kicking around a few ideas and hadn't quite landed on a name I liked. Then one day I was on the back of our Vespa with Mick driving. We were zipping through traffic, and it popped into my head: The Transit Lounge.

I yelled out to Mick, "What do you think about The Transit Lounge as a name? You know, everyone's always in transit, working towards a result, and it's great to have a place they can go to get extra support, guidance and direction on their journey?"

He said, "I like it."

So, The Transit Lounge it was.

The logo represents the simplicity, strength, determination and beauty of the lotus flower growing up through muddy water, opening to the sky, planting new seeds and growing again.

Why is mindset important?

I now think of mindset as the foundation of every part of life. It's what and how you think. It's like the gateway that allows you to see possibilities, access perspectives and ultimately influence your results.

The definition of mindset is: *a set of assumptions, attitudes and habits that influence your responses, decisions and behaviour.* It's what you believe to be true and possible for yourself.

The majority of the time people are almost completely unaware of what their mindset and beliefs are, until they're challenged or unmet in some way. It's critical to become more consciously aware of what your mindset is around certain areas of your life or work.

If you want to improve or change your results in any area, then you need to actively cultivate a mindset that models people who've already achieved the results you're aiming for. As an example, cultivating the mindset of being the CEO of Brand You will open up options, responsibilities and ideas you may not have seen if you didn't have that mindset.

Why is mindfulness important?

For me, mindfulness was a critical component of my recovery from severe adrenal fatigue and is now a part of my daily life. There's over thirty years of scientific research into the huge array of benefits of mindfulness, and it's now being adopted in businesses and industries across the world.

Google designed an entire mindfulness program that was initially offered as an internal learning and development program, and it rapidly became their most popular one. They now have an entire business called Search Inside Yourself, which runs a version of that program for other companies across the world.

There's no doubt in my mind the Google factor has had a major impact on the credibility of mindfulness, which I think is great. Research studies have shown mindfulness is beneficial in a huge number of areas, including focus, productivity, innovation, depression, stress reduction, creativity and decision making.

Over thirty years ago Jon Kabat-Zinn, widely regarded as the father of mindfulness, designed a program called Mindfulness Based Stress Reduction (MBSR). I decided to complete this program early in 2015. It challenged me and brought me a greater sense of awareness in regards to connecting to myself and my body in a way I hadn't experienced before.

Without mindfulness, people rush around reflecting, analysing and stewing in their juices about something that's already happened or stressing, worrying, and anticipating something that may not happen in the future. You're missing so much of life by not being present wherever you are.

My mindfulness teacher, Kate, said, "I want to live not just the length of this life, I want to live the width of it as well, and mindfulness allows me to do that." What a beautiful way to live life.

> "Mindfulness is the awareness and approach to life that arises from paying attention on purpose, being fully present with curiosity and compassion."
> ~Ed Halliwell

Jon Kabat-Zinn also talks about mindfulness as "a way of being". He says for this to happen, there needs to be a foundation to draw upon. If you want to run a marathon, you don't just rock up on the day it's happening and expect to be able to complete it. If you want to bring a greater sense of mindfulness and connection to yourself and your daily interactions with others, it takes a commitment to practicing those skills, so you can access them when you need them.

I incorporate elements of mindfulness into my coaching programs and some speaking gigs, as I truly believe it's a foundational element, no matter what aspect of life or work you're prioritising.

I also love how there are different types of mindfulness. I'm a Gemini, so I rarely like to have just one of anything. You already have the two most important tools you need to be mindful: your breath and your body. Whilst your mind is frequently not in the present moment, your body and breath always are, so you can use them any time you want to connect to the present.

Some of the formal practises include body scanning, breath work, open awareness, walking mindfulness, mindful eating, moving mindfulness practices, and cultivating compassion and loving kindness for yourself and others.

Shandra Moran

Why is money important?

This is an interesting one. I've always been a fan of money. I like having it, earning it, saving it and spending it. I'm lucky my parents instilled some good practices around money from an early age.

I had my first paying job when I was about fourteen. I worked at a local deli and then as a kitchen hand at a restaurant and function centre. The rule was that no matter how much, or how little, I earned, I had to pay a third to my parents as room and board, save a third and do whatever I wanted with the rest. At the time, I thought it was harsh. I realised later it was a good lesson about life and money. It set me up well for the reality of having to pay rent and expenses, and the importance of having a regular saving plan.

I'm also grateful to a drive announcer I worked with early in my radio career. My salary negotiation was coming up, and I was feeling a little nervous about it. He told me that the stronger I negotiated for myself, the more confident the company would be in my ability to negotiate strongly for them.

From that time on, I ensured my mindset was strong around negotiation and was generally happy with the results. I continue to stretch my comfort zone in conversations about money, keep building my beliefs around the value I provide and the compensation I receive in exchange.

When I was diagnosed with severe adrenal fatigue and decided I wanted to resign from my corporate gig, I was lucky I had a supportive husband. I was also in a financial position where I'd created enough of a money cushion to be able to maintain our lifestyle, which included servicing four mortgages.

The costs involved in focussing on my health and wellbeing were not insignificant.

I wondered what people who hit burnout or were ready for a new profession would do if they didn't have the financial backup. I was speaking to a friend about this, and she said' "They die earlier." It sounds a bit harsh, but at the same time there's a lot of truth in what she said. It upset and concerned me. I couldn't imagine being in my situation and having to continue pushing myself to stay at my job.

If I'd remained in my work situation, my health would have gotten far worse. It also breaks my heart every time I meet someone who has a true passion, and yet the work they do is completely disconnected from that. I know people who have a dream, a calling, and they continue to deny it, because they say they can't afford to leave their job. They're scared about not being able to make enough money doing what they love.

I've become quite fascinated with the concept of money, particularly in relation to women. I noticed that quite a few friends and clients had challenging relationships with it and would:

- have a level of debt they couldn't get on top of

- not negotiate strongly for themselves when it came to salary negotiation

- undercharge in their own business

- way over deliver

I believe in everyone pursuing their passion and making the world a better place because of it. After doing some research, I wound up becoming accredited as a Money Breakthrough Coach and realised how passionate I was about assisting, particularly women, to improve their relationship with money, so they no longer use it as an excuse for not making the choices they need to make.

Now I run programs designed to assist working women to do what they love and get highly paid for it. Awesome.

Why is meaningful work important?

This has always been an inherent belief of mine. When I fell into my radio career and felt like I'd found the perfect place for me, I loved it. I was good in that environment. For the most part I loved the people I worked with, as well as the variety. I had great success quickly and kept getting promoted.

My radio career was right for me for a time. And then it wasn't. I wanted something more, and I knew I had to make a choice between the comfort of staying in a job that wasn't allowing me to fully express who I was and all I had to offer, or risking it all to find something that would.

I chose the risk.

It led me to review what was most important to me in my career. What did I like doing? What did I seem to be good at? Would someone pay me to do it? The more I've been guided by my values and who I actually want to be, the more aligned I've felt to the work I'm doing, and generally the better the results I've had.

I believe everyone operates by a set of values that guide decision making and action. By seeking out and doing work you love and find meaningful, you'll be able to tap into your greatest energy, passion and abilities.

A job or career is supposed to evolve over time, and ideally it will be an expression of who you are and not just something you do for a pay cheque. That's soul destroying and energy sucking.

Find out what's most important to you, what your true values are, and then orient your life and work as an expression of that, even if you have to create a transition plan to get there.

So how do you figure out what your values are? Well, the clues are all around you. Your life up until now has been trying to show you your purpose. It's just that you're often so caught up worrying what other people think or scared of taking risks, that you ignore the signs. The best way to identify your values is to work with a coach who can do a values elicitation process with you. If you're not ready for that yet, you can start by reflecting on these questions:

- Where and on what do you spend most of your free time?
- If you were given a hundred dollars to spend on something you love, what would it be?
- What results have you achieved in any area of your life that you're most proud of?

Then you can consider what's most important to you. Is there a theme that runs through your answers to these questions? There's more to it, and this will at least get you started.

What's the best way to set and achieve goals?

To be honest, I never really set goals before I did my coach training, and even after that it took me a while to get into some sort of system or approach to it.

A quote I love is:

> "The bad news is, time flies. The good news is, you are the pilot"
> ~Michael Altshuler

Goal setting helps you make the best use of the time that's going to just keep flying past. The best way is to start by creating and connecting to a big vision. As the CEO of Brand You, what do you want to create in your life? Write down in as much detail as possible what a happy, healthy, prosperous, and inspiring life would look like for you.

This can be quite confronting when you start, because you might think you don't know, but I believe you do. It's just hidden behind stories or beliefs that you can't have it or don't deserve it, so you keep playing it safe and small.

I encourage you to go somewhere beautiful, for instance by the water or to a park. Just get out of your usual space and open up to the big, beautiful world around you. It helps ideas to flow.

I like to choose a word of the year that sums up what I'd most like to be or grow into. This acts as a great focus tool when different opportunities and ideas come along. It helps to quickly check in and ask myself, *Is this going to move me closer or farther away from living my word of the year?*

Once you have your word, choose up to three focus areas of your life to set goals for. Don't have any more than three, otherwise it will be too much, and that makes it difficult to get momentum going.

The strongest goals will be an expression of your highest values. They're the ones you're most likely to feel inspired by and follow through on.

When you write a goal, make sure it's:

- stated in the positive, what you do want, not what you don't
- within your control and not reliant on someone else
- something tangible with a specific timeframe, so you'll know when you've achieved it.

I always recommend you share your goals with a partner, friend or some sort of mentoring group. This brings a new level of accountability and increases the level of support you will have, as well as the likelihood of following through and taking action.

Then you have to keep your goals top of mind and take micro actions towards them every day. Yes it's an investment of time, but if you're someone who really wants to be the CEO and pilot of your own life, then this is the best way to get into that big seat at the front of the plane.

Do you have a morning routine that sets the tone for your day?

I have a beautiful morning routine. This has developed over the last two years or so, and I love it.

When I get up I have a big glass of water. It's important to hydrate. Then I turn on some little lights we bought in Kho Samui that are carved out of coconut shells, and I put a beautiful essential oil in my vaporiser.

I prepare a glass of warm water with fresh lemon juice and apple cider vinegar and sip it. Then I lay out my yoga mat and towel. If the weather is good I do it outside, or if not, I put it next to our gigantic Himalayan salt lamp and do a short yoga or meridian stretching sequence, followed by a mindfulness practise. I like variety, so I mix up what type I do. Sometimes it's a standing movement practice or a lying down body scan. I finish by setting my intention and focus for the day. Once I've done that, I make a healthy breakfast that might consist of a green smoothie, eggs, or gluten-free cereal and herbal tea.

Then I shower and get ready for the day.

What was the one thing that when you got it, everything else seemed to fall into place?

Again, being a Gemini, I'm going to choose two. The biggest one was the concept of being the boss of me. Of all the people I encounter who will love and care for me, I'm the only one who will be with me for my whole life. It was a big epiphany when I realised this was true. I'm the CEO of my own life, and therefore I'm responsible for everything that does and doesn't happen, and how I respond.

The other is that it's not about getting it right, it's about having a go.

This isn't an excuse for poor delivery or performance. It's about getting out of your own way and not waiting for circumstances to be perfect before you take action. In all likelihood there's never a perfect time, and waiting around for it could serve as an excellent excuse to never get started as you continue to shop your story around of all reasons you would have, should have, could have, and yet *didn't* take action.

As soon as you can get over these obstacles and just get started, the situation changes. A great teacher from my early coach training, Joe Pane, told a story about mother ducks. You know the saying, *Once I get all my ducks in a row*? Well, you don't really see mother ducks running around trying to round up all of their little ducklings before they decide to go somewhere. The mother duck starts moving, and all of the ducklings scurry into line and follow her. So as often as possible, I want to be the mother duck moving in the direction I want to go while trusting that the momentum it creates will provide insights into what to do next.

How do you currently make a difference in people's lives?

I'm back in alignment, doing the work I'm supposed to be doing, which is helping people to be their best, authentic self. It's all based around the concept of creating true wellbeing: the contented state of feeling happy, healthy and prosperous. I do private coaching, workshops and online programs, and I'll be running retreats and mastermind groups. I offer a range of options, because some people love group workshops, while others don't feel comfortable in a group situation and prefer private sessions. There are people who want to partner over the long term, while others want a shorter, immersive experience.

I'm quite an eclectic coach and facilitator, as I draw on a wide range of experience, training and study, and I'll use any tools or techniques I think will best serve the client to achieve the result they're looking for.

I also believe that by doing this work, it shows there's a way back from being burnt out. If I can do it, you can, too. It's important for me to walk the talk and continue to learn and grow by applying what I've learned and sharing it with others.

 To discover more about how Shandra can help you *Elevate Your Success*, visit

www.elevate-books.com/success

David Coe
The Bandits' Gift

David Coe, Australia's authority on investor social media, is a communications strategist who has the rare ability to write for the head and the heart.

He combines the discipline of a career in financial journalism and investment banking with insights gained from thirty-five years of study into human behaviour in such diverse places as a Buddhist monastery, Sydney, Queensland and Cambridge universities, Findhorn in Scotland, the schools of Werner Erhard and John Demartini, and the newsrooms of more than a dozen major newspapers around the world.

David is an accomplished presenter, author, editor, animation producer, and script writer who quickly gets to the intellectual and emotional core of a business case.

He is the managing editor of his own firm, Investor Torque, which helps junior listed companies reach tens of thousands of investors on social media.

Please visit David's company website, investortorque.com or his personal website, davidcoe.com.au for more information.

David Coe

The Bandits' Gift

What major experience has shaped your life?

Ignoring my inner wisdom almost cost me my life.

While hitchhiking in thirty-nine degree heat across northern Spain to get to the Running of the Bulls festival, I was dropped at a junction of two major highways. Only a sleepy hamlet was nearby, so no cars would come from there. I was in the best position to get my next ride.

But my intuition was clear. "Move, David," it said. "Move."

My logic kicked in, and it told me there was no reason to move.

I was definitely in the best position near the junction on a dual carriageway. The sweltering heat made carrying my backpack decidedly taxing, and besides, where was I going to walk to?

As I pondered what to do, I heard it again.

"Move, David," my intuition said.

My logic countered, "Where to?"

For half an hour as I baked in the sun, my intuition and logic fought in a mental tug-of-war.

"Move, David."

"Where to?"

The Bandits' Gift

Then I noticed a young man in a picnic area on the edge of the hamlet about 200m away. He was in his late teens or early twenties and was soon joined by a mate.

"Move, David."

"Where to?"

I was uneasy about the pair of them, but the trouble now was that they were between me and the hamlet.

"Move, David."

"Where to?"

They were joined by a third friend, then a fourth and a fifth.

My unease turned to anxiety, and my intuition became insistent.

"Move, David."

But my logic was confused, uncertain: "Where to?"

Then they started to move—towards me. Now there was no way of getting to the hamlet beyond them.

Within minutes, they were in a semi-circle around me, tugging at my backpack as I stood on the edge of the dual carriageway.

"*Pasaporte, dinero.*"

They wanted my passport and money.

Then one of the bandits pulled a stiletto knife as long as his forearm out of his shirt sleeve and said again, "*Pasaporte, dinero.*"

David Coe

The next thing I knew, my backpack and I were landing on the white line between the lanes of the dual carriageway about 3m from where I'd been standing, where the stiletto had been pulled on me.

I looked up to see a car in each lane closing in on me at 100km/h. There was a *whoosh, whoosh* as they veered just centimetres on either side of me. They scattered the bandits.

One of the cars stopped, reversed back, and carried me away to safety. As I sat in the back seat reflecting on my ordeal and rescue, I couldn't work out if I'd jumped over the bandits or ran between them or if I had a fairy godmother who plucked me out of there. My memory went blank after the stiletto was pulled.

As I pondered my near-death experience, my logic said to my intuition, "From now on, you show me what you know," and I made a promise to myself that I would listen to my intuition and act on it

What's the best thing that has ever happened to you and why?

Learning to act on my intuition—my inner wisdom—was a lesson that would pay dividends years later when my logic-based career was at a crossroads.

In the 1970s I'd been trained as a finance journalist on a Brisbane newspaper. I did it in a cadetship, which is the classic method.

They were the days of hot metal and typewriters. An extra carbon copy of everything the other cadets and I wrote was sent to our cadet mentor, a former chief sub-editor who went through it line by line, word by word. He used his decades of experience in the cauldron of daily journalism to teach us how to get to the point immediately, how to structure stories, and how to make every word count. We learnt how to write with the discipline of a samurai and how to use the pen like a sword.

That intense training in news gathering, accuracy, word craft, punctuation and grammar was arguably the best thing that happened to me in my career. After all, it laid the foundation for me to become the features editor of one of New Zealand's main newspapers by the age of twenty two, and to work in London on both *The Times* and *The Sun* by my mid-twenties. This training also taught me a much more subtle, but equally valuable, lesson, and that was the value of a coach. Elite sportspeople and teams wouldn't dream of competing without a coach. High-flying business people with a commitment to success often take coaches. Most people don't see the value of having one, and neither would I if I hadn't trained under one. I also would not have been able to pass on the lessons I learnt and help thousands of people over the years make their words sparkle.

What have been some of your life-changing decisions?

By 2009, after I'd been the editor on the *Financial Review* responsible for its information graphics and charts for seven years, a thought began to gnaw away at me. The team of graphic artists I was responsible for was producing world-class work day in and day out to capture the important elements of major stories, yet my intuition told me something I couldn't quite decipher.

I looked back on previous successes at Macquarie Bank, which included creating a document that brought in $12 million in share sales in its first two weeks. I also redesigned Macquarie's equities research, and fund managers voted it their third most used research reports after it had previously been unranked. I'd even redesigned the business section of *The Australian* before that.

Yet my gnawing thought left me dissatisfied.

Then I realised my intuition was telling me it was time to take on new challenges. It would not let me rest on my laurels. I had to walk away from a regular salary and risk going into business for myself. Getting a job on another newspaper or at another bank was not the answer. It would have meant similar dissatisfaction in new surroundings.

Journalists can be professional fence-sitters who never take a stand and spend their lives writing about what other people do. I had to get off the fence and take action. The risk of working the next fifteen years to retirement was that I would get to the end of my career disappointed in myself for playing it safe and eventually die with a song still inside of me.

As the saying goes, we regret only those things we didn't do.

However, there were a few basic problems. I didn't know what that song sounded like, and I didn't know how to build a business. There was a lot I didn't know.

So it was time to get a coach.

I wanted to maximise my growth, and that meant dealing with my weaknesses. Lucky for me, good coaches can see into our blind spots, where our weaknesses usually lie.

I found a firm of career consultants and for twelve months planned my escape from salaried employment. I learnt how to work the non-advertised job market, where seventy percent of jobs are found. I wanted clients, not employers, but the principles are the same. I learnt to network properly instead of just turning up at an event and trying to sell my services to anyone who would listen. I learnt how to construct an elevator pitch that showcased my value and which I could deliver with heartfelt honesty and authenticity.

By the time I left the *Financial Review,* almost twelve months to the day I had begun up-skilling myself, I had five coaches. One for business, one for marketing, one for technical analysis of markets, one for trading futures, and one for personal communications. I also took courses on social media, small business and public speaking.

Have you had any aha moments that changed everything for you?

At the same time all of this was going on, there was a crucial moment I realised a truth that had been blindingly obvious throughout my career in both financial journalism and investment banking: both the business press and stock brokers cover only companies with the most shares, the most customers, the most employees and the biggest effect on the economy. Of the two-thousand companies on the Australian Securities Exchange, only about two hundred get much coverage. It's as if the rest shout into an empty room when they release their announcements.

As I slowly pieced together the jigsaw of skills needed to be the CEO of my own life, I noticed the convergence of three trends, and then I began to see my skill set in a new light. These are the three trends, which have since intensified:

1. Newspapers are shrinking as their advertising revenue dries up, which means it has never been harder for junior companies to get publicity.

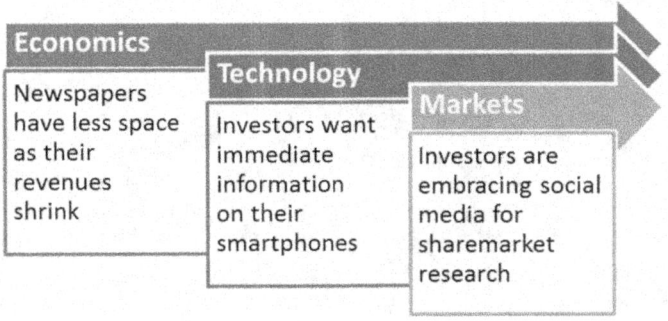

2. Investors want information immediately, and smartphones have put the internet into people's pockets.

3. Investors who trade online, manage their portfolios online and research online are embracing social media as an alternative to expensive news feeds like Bloomberg and Reuters.

The convergence of the three trends means companies can reach investors with valuable information direct through social media. Junior companies have been freed from the necessity of traditional coverage.

However, the biggest mistake companies make when trying to use social media to reach investors is to unthinkingly adopt a consumer social media model. After all, an iron ore company doesn't sell more iron to a steel mill because of its Facebook page, and a biotech company working on a cure for cancer doesn't even have a product to sell.

Being successful in investor social media takes mastery of three skills:

1. Journalism skills are needed to craft posts on social media in ways that engage investors, because companies mistakenly think Australian Securities Exchange announcements are the only communications worth sending to investors.

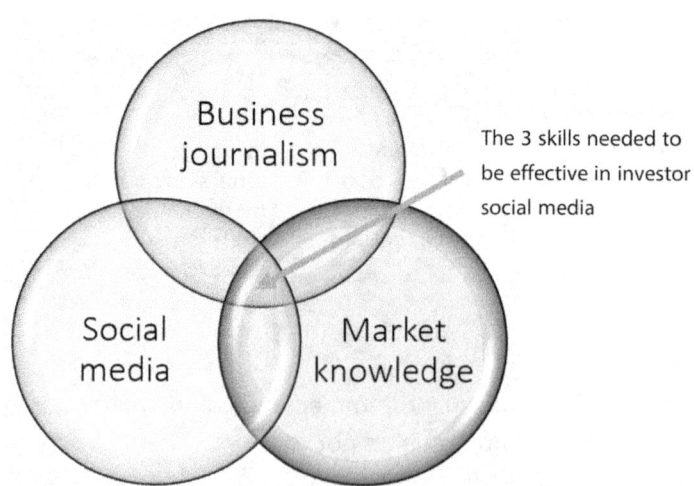

The 3 skills needed to be effective in investor social media

2. Market knowledge is needed to know how investors think, what they value and what's important, and to talk to them with the right level of assumed knowledge.

3. Social media skills are needed to use the new platforms effectively, to find people who value market information, to engage them with information they value, and to provide information in formats that suit the channels on which it's posted.

Few people have mastered all three skill sets. Those who know social media are often too young to have much market experience, while those with decades of market experience have rarely been trained to write to professional standards. Most journalists have little idea how to run a social media campaign.

What's your most inspiring story about a client?

When all three skills come together, the results can be astounding.

One client, a junior gold company that was about to transition from explorer to producer by pouring its first ever gold bars, had a problem. Corporate raiders were trying to oust the board and take control of the company on the eve of the gold pour, which was expected to send the share price soaring.

Instead of launching a normal takeover and paying a premium for the shares, the raiders called an extraordinary meeting to have shareholders vote out the incumbent directors and replace them with the raiders. The company needed to mobilise shareholders and make them aware of the skulduggery, in order to vote down the raiders. Using social media, we were able to get the full story to between 50,000 and 115,000 investors, stock brokers, analysts, wealth advisers, fund managers, corporate finance executives, asset consultants, business journalists and others every two weeks in the run-up to the shareholder meeting.

Our efforts worked, and the shareholders rejected the raiders. The incumbent board maintained control and was able to oversee the first gold pour, which produced income for the company.

Another client, a financial services company, used social media to take news of its new contracts and rising profitability direct to the market. In the process, it increased the number of its shares sold each day from an average of 100,000 to 400,000 after its investor social media campaign began.

This increase in share liquidity validates a Stanford University study into the power of social media, which shows that when companies use it to amplify their announcements, they reach more investors. The more buyers and sellers there are, the smaller the gap between the price buyers are offering and the price sellers are asking, which in turn makes getting into and out of a stock less risky. Investors like strong turnover and are generally more willing to invest in companies with strong turnover and narrow spreads between buyers and sellers. In three months, our client's share price more than doubled.

Another client, a micro-cap copper explorer, lifted its turnover tenfold from two million shares a month to twenty million after using social media to reach investors with news of its successes.

It's results like these that reinforce my passion for social media's ability to transform the way companies communicate with investors. Cultivating followers who value market information and giving them the information means they make our clients' messages go viral. That results in our clients no longer having to suffer in silence. Instead, they're known, heard and understood by investors.

We've had clients retweeted by a Warren Buffett company, stock brokers, TV news presenters, fund managers, and ASX news portals, as well as institutional investors. Our record for the most people a client reached in a single retweet is 410,000.

Social media is also powerful in alerting investors to prospectuses, information memorandums and investor presentations. Including links to the documents makes it easy for investors to click through to them on your website.

One client, an iron ore developer, presented at an investor conference. Only 120 people were in the room to hear the managing director speak, yet almost 5,000 investors saw his presentation on social media.

Other clients who have prospectuses for retail investors and information memorandums for sophisticated investors, have had hundreds of click-throughs and downloads during campaigns to raise capital.

Social media's ability to reach the markets direct means companies can combine it with their offline strategies to create synergies that deliver on their business objectives.

What other mistakes do people make regarding investor social media?

Social media is word of mouth on steroids. This is why my company is called Investor Torque. It plays on the idea that talk is a powerful marketing tool. However, a second mistake people make when they try to adopt a consumer social media model to reach investors is to focus only on increasing the number of followers. It can lead into the trap of buying followers who don't value your content. Even if companies don't buy followers, they must do more than just attract lots of followers.

Companies need followers who will share their posts and value the companies' information. It enables companies to tap into the networks of their followers. It's how they can go viral and reach unique investors. Followers who don't care about your content won't share it or talk about it. Nor will they act upon it. Your investment in social media will be wasted.

A third common mistake companies make is to talk just about themselves. Investors love information about forces affecting the sector, and therefore their investment. On the other hand, directors and executives often know a lot of specialised information in the public domain they could share but don't. When companies only talk about themselves, they're cutting off a wider audience. This is particularly true for companies raising capital and are tempted to talk just about their offer.

The analogy of a cocktail party is appropriate here. Someone standing in the middle of the room talking about themselves may engage only one or two people, while someone talking about topics of interest to others has a small crowd surrounding them.

One more mistake companies make is to overlook the power of LinkedIn for highlighting management's skills and expertise. Ask yourself this question: when you invest, do you care about the quality of a company's management? Of course you do, and so do other investors.

It's unfortunate that a common attitude among old-school directors and executives is to focus only on personal meetings and leave their LinkedIn profile almost blank, if they have one at all. A strong profile that reflects your experience, even what you've learned from previous setbacks, will help attract investors to your company. They will have greater faith in your ability to steward their investment.

The most powerful strategy is to use your online profile to bolster your offline efforts. Think about the number of times you've looked up someone online just before or after meeting them. Other people look you up online as well. For instance, those who might consider investing in your company you'll never meet in person.

How you appear online tells the world who you are, so don't waste the opportunity to highlight your value, or worse, undermine your own credibility with a shoddy profile. Consider having a professional write your profile in order to get the strongest result and leave you free to concentrate on what you do best.

How are you currently making a difference in people's lives?

When an investor social media campaign with clear business objectives is implemented properly, everyone benefits. Shareholders get information they value, the company gets its message to the markets, investors are attracted, liquidity increases, spreads tighten, and directors and management are valued more highly.

Making this sort of difference inspires us at Investor Torque. It's our purpose for doing what we do.

For me, personally, I'm grateful for the chance to show companies the power of social media to reach investors. It offers companies opportunities beyond traditional investor communications. It also offers opportunities beyond traditional media for our team of editors that stretches from London to Melbourne.

When companies discover social media offers them much more than celebrities drumming up attention for themselves or people wasting time on Facebook, I know I'm making a difference to them, and the people who depend on them, such as staff, management, families, customers, and suppliers. When they discover they no longer have to shout their announcements into an empty room and can talk directly to investors, I feel as if I'm fulfilling a higher purpose.

Creating communications that pay dividends is my calling, and it's as if I'm living out my life purpose by helping companies be heard, known and understood.

Though it would be easy to look back at my successes in journalism, investment banking or investor social media and mistakenly think my career unfolded smoothly and without challenge or error, I believe we learn our biggest lessons from our mistakes. Journalists in particular have a piece of black humour that reminds them of the consequences of their mistakes.

Doctors' mistakes may die, but journalists' mistakes live on in print. I cringe when I remember some of my mistakes. They're called clangers in the trade. Even the small mistakes had lessons. When I started in journalism I misspelled names, because I was embarrassed to ask questions with apparently obvious answers. Is it John Brown or Jon Browne? Lotus Creek or Loaders Creek?

Years later, I can say the mistake with the biggest consequences was when an error in an Excel spreadsheet lead to newspapers being pulped and reprinted, because a data table about Australia's biggest companies was simply wrong.

What's a strategy you can recommend for living life powerfully?

Throughout my career, all errors stung me into re-evaluating myself. It was not enough to let embarrassment stop me from making a fool of myself at the expense of accuracy. It was not enough to blame a team member's oversight with Excel. Responsibility rested with me, and I had to be big enough to accept that responsibility. This meant elevating my thinking.

When we feel gutted, and I felt gutted every time a mistake appeared in print, we're tempted to think small, to be small. To hide from the world. But that's the dead end of a small life that can only get smaller. The most powerful response is to accept increasing amounts of responsibility. Think of it as the ability to respond, which leads to a rich life of variety, challenge, results and fulfilment.

Let me give you a practical example. If you ride a motorcycle safely in Sydney, it requires taking an extraordinary degree of responsibility. As I ride my 600cc Honda from meeting to meeting, or even casually on weekends, I ride as if I'm invisible to every other vehicle. I give myself the ability to respond no matter the situation. If a car has to give me right of way at a roundabout or intersection, I look to see if its wheels start to turn, because that can be seen before movement is noticeable and gives me time to stop. I also look in the driver's eyes, because if I can't see them, there's a good chance he can't see me and won't give me right of way.

This ability to respond was tested soon after I joined one of Australia's top daily newspapers in the 1990s. My line manager, the chief sub-editor of the section, told me plainly, "David, I don't like you, I don't trust you, and if I had my way you'd be out the door."

Coincidentally I'd been doing a course on taking a hundred percent responsibility for the quality of my relationships, and this was going to be the ideal one on which to practise. I had to elevate my thinking and recognise her commitment to the newspaper, while firmly and quietly sharing my commitment. Descending into a slanging match would only entrench the conflict and exacerbate the tension. Eventually I was promoted and no longer answerable to her. As I was leaving four years later, she made a point of seeking me out to say, "We will miss you. Good luck."

Why is mindset important?

When you elevate your thinking, you elevate your life. It's because thoughts become words that become things. Or to put it another way, what you think about comes about.

Elevating your life is impossible with the wrong mindset. Too often we fall into the trap of thinking that if we're not getting the results we want, we have to continue our actions with more power, more force, more intensity.

But that's just more of the same. As the saying goes, doing the same things over and over and expecting different results is the definition of insanity. The key to elevating your thinking and elevating your life is to adopt a growth mindset. This doesn't mean thinking positively. Trying to think positively just results in depression, because everywhere you look you will see what isn't positive. That is the paradox we have to live inside.

It's much better to see there's positive and negative, and support and challenge, in everything. For example, the better the time you have on holiday, the more disappointing it is to come home. Another example is looking back and laughing at past setbacks. Tragedies can become comedies over time. A growth mindset sees hiccups, hurdles and obstacles as part of the path to success, not in the way of it. A growth mindset sees every challenge as an opportunity to learn and grow. After all, when we're green, we grow, and when we're ripe, we rot.

A growth mindset allows you to overcome human emotional wounds, which is critical to using intuition. This is because using intuition requires you to be present, so you can see how this moment will unfold.

Emotional wounds cause you to regret the past or fear the future. You could say we don't have emotions—emotions have us. Those emotions distort intuition, because they take you out of the present and put you in the past or the future. So be present. All of your power exists there.

The highest form of elevated thinking is to love yourself. That doesn't mean being infatuated but to value yourself enough to nurture your own growth. The Buddha once gave a great example to illustrate love. He said the difference between liking something and loving something can be seen in a flower. If we like a flower, we simply pick it. If we love it, we water and tend it. When you elevate your thinking, you effectively upgrade the way you think, tap your intuition, and build your skills in the physical world. Elevated thinking allows you to create an empowering context in which to live, love and work.

To discover more about how David can help you *Elevate Your Success*, visit

www.elevate-books.com/success

Kim Walker

Resilience To Brilliance

With thirty years as a world-class peak performer, Kim has enjoyed a prolific career as an international soloist with thirty-three prize-winning CDs. She also has twenty years of experience as a senior leader and professor in higher education.

Kim's brand-new signature program, the Virtuoso Factor, has been refined while working on six continents in five languages with university presidents, international performers, politicians, CEOs, educators, performers and professionals.

Kim is the founder and owner of VirtuosoCEO, which is a boutique consulting company that mentors leaders, business owners and their teams to reinvent, design and deliver game-changing results that leave a legacy of distinction.

In recent years, Kim has been responsible for generating sponsorship in excess of $123 million for her clients. Indiana University Press is publishing her first book, *Spirited Wind Playing*, which is about peak performance and mindset. As speaker, coach and consultant, Kim delivers simple and proven ways for CEO leadership teams and performing arts organizations to orchestrate growth.

Kim Walker

Resilience To Brilliance

This beautiful world can be a tough old taskmistress. Everyone needs to develop attributes that will enable them to survive "the slings and arrows of outrageous fortune." A measure of resilience is vital, but it's really about how you make use of the heat and pressure to deliver diamonds. There's no road map for how to get from *resilience to brilliance*, but the journey isn't as difficult as you might think, and the possible rewards are beyond your wildest dreams.

It's first about *being* a great person and then about what you do and how you do it.

Here's a true story about Pablo Picasso. He was admiring his friend and rival Matisse's masterpiece, the stained glass windows in the *Chapelle du Rosaire* in Venice, when he said, "You're crazy to make a chapel for those people!" Matisse's response was, "You're like me. What we both search for in art is the climate of our first communion." As Picasso protested, Matisse asked, "Where does the art come from?"

Have you ever questioned your life purpose?

Musicians know their purpose early in life, or so it would seem. My first world was music. We learn that to be a champion requires a technique with the precision of a neurosurgeon, the daring of a bullfighter, the training of an elite athlete and the mindset of a black belt master. Years of disciplined, daily improvement, analysis and practice are needed to develop the ability to confront the nerve-wracking world of peak performance and deliver the ultimate in extreme situations.

Regularly preparing for and performing to audiences large and small on six continents instils the key lessons of leadership. You have to learn that the standing ovations and the harsh criticisms are just opposite sides of the same coin. It's all part of the game. The real test is how you avoid being diverted by the ego-driven judgments of others and concentrate on developing your own strengths. That's the virtuoso factor of focusing on the music. Musicians enjoy moments of pure ecstasy, which are unparalleled orgasmic bliss, punctuated by long, long periods of soul-testing, finger-dazzling, brain-teasing practice. And more practice. And then more practice, because the risks are high and the rewards are spectacular.

But life wasn't always so easy. Like all musicians, I know that moment of wondering if anyone would ever hire me, playing on the streets for petty cash and practicing without any guarantee but my own self-belief and tenacity.

I've always loved skiing and climbing. One day, almost twenty-five years ago, my friends and I were in Switzerland climbing an especially steep 4,092m peak called Pollux. All of a sudden, I felt my foot slip a few inches. My heart leapt as I held on and stood. Then a surreal vision appeared. Hans-Walter, our guide, lost his grip and fell just above me. Time almost stopped as I watched his airborne descent and considered our options. In that split second, all four of us who were tied onto the same rope began sliding down the mountain. I'd heard of this happening and seen it in films, but at the time I wondered how it could be happening to me.

I used every ounce of energy I had to dig in the ice axe and halt our fall. Then I felt and saw it. More euphoric, compelling and gentle than anything I had ever known, the white tunnel of light appeared and was drawing me in toward the central orb. Each blissful microsecond felt like the verge of climax. Warm arms of light enveloped me with timeless grace. I was weightless. Ahead was pure energy, light and the source of everything. I've never been so happy or in such a state of bliss and calmness.

At the same time, I saw my parents. I was aware of exactly where they were sitting, what they were wearing at home in New York, as well as my West Highland terriers down in Zermatt. It was gut-wrenching to know how devastated my parents would be, and in this space I asked myself, *How can I let them know I'm okay*? I was in a beautiful, even sublime, space, when out of nowhere I heard a deep voice say, *"Have you done everything you came here to do?"* I wondered who was talking to me and how it was so clear. Jolted, I looked around and only saw white light. Again the voice asked the question, loud and clear. Without a thought I answered, *No, I haven't even begun.*

Then, boom, I was back in the present, sliding and thrashing, fighting with every ounce of my being. We were hurtling down, bumping into each other and being tossed around. Then it eased and ceased. A weightless dread engulfed me, as I became aware that I was now falling *into* the mountain. I landed softly in a bowl of powdered snow, and my friend, Jane landed next to me. She said, "Kim, are we dead or alive?" I answered, "I don't know, but if we're talking to each other, I guess we're still alive."

Hans-Walter fell in a heap and groaned, while Roger flew through the air like a human missile, unconscious, with his hands held peacefully down by his sides. Then he hit a huge piece of ice and rolled toward us. Wondering where we were, I looked down by my side. Two inches to my right was a cavern at least a mile deep, with intense marbled blue veins of ice. I was sitting in the belly of a crevasse. A shiver went through me when I realised the bridge of snow we were on would melt within minutes. In fact, it was a miracle it was supporting us.

Roger was turning blue and needed to be resuscitated. The primordial scream he let out when finally able to breathe is unforgettable. I vowed to myself that we would all survive the blizzard that was still raging, get out of the crevasse and make it home again.

Safety depended on quickly moving out of danger, with what I call the 3 C's: *clarity* to identify what was needed, *confidence* to bring real, heart-centred focus and *courage* to dare to go beyond fear. Two of our party were hurt, and it was unclear if they could walk. In a concert, when performers are nervous and stressed and things go wrong, a conductor utilises the three C's, along with a few magic ego pills, to get a group moving forward in one unified direction.

I knew that in order to survive we had to tap into the 3 C's and get down off the mountain before nightfall. Clarity was based on an intuitive sense of the physical realities, a rough assessment of the mindset and energy of the team, and whatever help a compass, an altimeter and a map could give us. Raising the energy and setting a positive mindset with focus and intent was vital to getting all of us safely through the next nine hours. Connecting with that light I'd seen was also essential. Visibility was nil, as we navigated a glacier crossed with more crevasses. Each time I prayed to the heavens, as if on cue the clouds miraculously parted for a split second, showing a clear passage. Survival depended on asking for help, staying full of the same energy I had just experienced and above all, letting go of my former preconceptions to allow all of us to be guided.

In this extreme situation, I experienced a direct, conscious connection with what I call *Source*, meaning the place we come from when a spark of life-force brings us into being. Until that moment, I'd had a vague awareness of it, but I hadn't realised I could communicate with it so directly. It was all so simple, I was left wondering how often our eyes and ears filter or block this connection.

I had a momentary insight into the deepest truth of who we are and what life is all about. How could I ever recapture it? How was that voice so clear? If I hadn't even begun, then what I was here to do? I was always someone who believed in music and a vibrant life. I wasn't interested in defining God or the goddess or Oneness or the Spirit, so this was a disturbing, yet intoxicating, new awareness. In that moment

I realised the rest of my life was a gift and that fearlessness is the key to making the most of every moment.

You experienced heightened consciousness and deeper awareness while you were on that mountain. Did you retain that same feeling in everyday life?

That life-changing experience on the mountain proved to me that tapping into a higher level of consciousness is possible. Slowly, with practice, I've learnt how to do this consistently for myself. Now one of my missions in life is helping others do the same.

Fast forward twenty-five years. The advantage of beginning your professional life at a precociously young age is that you can enjoy several careers. I've been a leader in music as a global performer, in education as dean and a professor in major research universities and in business as Founder and CEO of VirtuosoCEO.

Experiencing conscious awareness is a cornerstone of my *VirtuosoCEO*™ program, in which I encourage Aussie CEOs to crash through the glass ceiling, and break a few records along the way, to achieve the accelerated growth they deserve. The lessons of leadership for artists, teachers, mountaineers or entrepreneurs are really quite similar. The link between survival and creativity is primary.

World-class performance in music, or any other field of endeavour, requires the 3 Cs of leadership:

- CLARITY to identify what you're willing to fight for and the skills needed to achieve the growth desired in the shortest amount of time.

- CONFIDENCE, because you have to be the first person to believe in your ability to succeed. If you can't convince yourself, you won't dispel anyone else's doubts.

▸ COURAGE in daring to go way beyond your comfort zone and continue through the finish line with commitment, passion, purpose and diligence.

What's important to remember when dealing with the unexpected?

I had no forewarning, no premonition of that cataclysmic slide down the mountain in Switzerland. If I had, I would have prepared for it. But sometimes life catches you unawares. When this happens, it's natural to be distracted and start obsessing about what you could have done to prevent it. This is a waste of time. True leaders may analyse what happened and take steps to prevent it in the future, but when the chips are down, they focus on action.

When there's loss of focus, the ego gets upset over the lack of perfection, and even more mistakes appear. Whatever you do, it's essential to balance the emotional pendulum. Neither euphoria nor depression provides a balanced view of any situation. Suppressing your blackest thoughts and deeds and hiding them from others is just as dangerous as announcing and sharing your excuses.

On stage you're fully exposed. As a bassoonist, if I crack a note or even achieve it without finesse, there's no hiding. An apology would only make it worse, because it would attract attention to the flaw. It's no different in any other field of endeavour. Learning to suspend judgment, to accept and use the energy of the moment, is what separates the good from the great. If you can embrace, accept and make use of all the pieces of your inner psyche, then even your dark side can help to create true awareness and range.

You won't know when these life challenges are going to arise, so you have to be ready to meet them at any time. These are the tests of leadership, whether in a boardroom, on stage or in the Olympic stadium. The tools you need to achieve your goals are the same: health, a strong mindset and a confidence cocktail grounded in full awareness.

The greatest leaders finish a task and move on to the next. The only real danger, the real pain, comes from holding on to resentment, anger, shame and blame. As the old saying goes, *Resentment is like swallowing poison and hoping the other person will die.* Don't internalise problems. Get them out in the open, deal with them appropriately, do whatever needs to be done and move on.

In the mountains, the weather can change without warning. A beautiful, sunny day can be wiped out by a thunderstorm before you can find shelter. In the world of finance, unforeseen catastrophes can wipe billions of dollars off share values. You have to be prepared to deal with the unexpected. In challenging situations, you often need to tap into your greatest and/or least attractive, strengths in order to help those around you.

In any field, CLARITY about the present, coupled with the COURAGE to dare to be different builds the CONFIDENCE you need to achieve success.

How do you achieve peak performance?

If you find it difficult to connect to your inner self when you're stressed and your mind works overtime on trivia when you want to focus on the big picture, or if your business is eroding your physical and mental health, then isn't it time you started using some proven skills and tools to regulate your stress levels more effectively, so you can reach your peak performance levels faster and easier?

Business problems can erode health. The key to mental health in business is learning how to regulate stress effectively, efficiently and quickly, so you can return to conscious awareness. Being nervous is normal whenever peak performance is part of the game. Musicians and athletes are trained in the key skills to succeed in high-pressure situations.

Everyone is different, so while meditations that still the mind or bring energy back to your body are helpful, there are many other approaches that work. Some have been taught for thousands of years, while others have been generated by the latest neuroscientific research. What's important is that every individual entering a competitive arena is armed with abilities and techniques that will help them to survive and succeed, in order to progress from *resilience to brilliance*.

Some people prefer medication to meditation. Some use diet and exercise, enjoy conversations or rely on the adrenalin rush of drama, which can drive less confident opponents straight back into their shells. The greatest antidote I know for high-pressure stress, nerves and the fear you feel when stretching beyond your comfort zone, is expert preparation and breathing deep into your centre to still the mind to a calm and yet productive space.

To put it in business terms, when there's too much information you can go into overwhelm. Perceived danger brings on stress, which releases a powerful hormone called cortisol that has the ability to wipe out fifty percent of your intellect in seven minutes. Cortisol inhibits your body's ability to digest proteins and restricts brain power while delivering known carcinogens into your system that can do untold damage.

When stressed or nervous, adrenaline and cortisol flood your system, reaching all of the extremities in your body. Almost instantly, there's an extra reserve of energy that prepares you for fight or flight. This explains how your ancestors were able to run fast for a short amount of time to get away from predators. Unfortunately, the cortisol remains in the system for over twenty-four hours. If stress restricts blood flow to your vital organs often enough or for long enough, your oxygen supply, hydration, nutrition and elimination abilities all wind up impaired.

Stress is designed to allow you to achieve superhuman feats in quick bursts. The downside is that it inhibits your ability to evaluate the danger. In order to win or increase the probability of success in business, learning how to manage and limit the effects of stress greatly increases the odds in your favour.

How do you manage stress in life and business?

DHEA is a natural de-stressor.

The antidote to stress, biologically and chemically, is simple: express gratitude with powerful sincerity and reclaim your natural resilience. Have you ever just melted when feeling truly grateful? When you're experiencing gratitude, your body creates and releases a neural hormone called DHEA, which lowers your cortisol level and helps your body recover from stress. So how do you get to gratitude when feeling agitated?

There are a number of ancient methods that use breathing techniques to align the mind and body and regain your balance, so you can raise your consciousness again.

Navy Seals will tell you that in a life-and-death situation, the person they trust most to get everyone out alive is the one who knows how to breathe consciously. There are many methods, but here's a simple one:

Begin by exhaling. Lower your jaw to expel that last bit of stale air. When you're ready, breathe in for a count of four seconds, hold the air in four seconds, exhale for four seconds and wait four more. How does that feel? Are you more in control of the moment?

If you find this idea inspiring, it's probably because the Latin meaning of the word inspiration is *breathing in*.

What is intuition or connecting with the Source?

That moment on the mountain has inspired me to spend many years studying neuroscience, psychology, business leadership, personal development and spiritual leaders. I've had the privilege of working with original thinkers worldwide who each have their own way of connecting to the Source, although they have many different ways of defining it, both spiritual and psychological.

The brain's prefrontal cortex is where I experienced that connection to the Source that saved all of us on the mountain that day. This is the same part of the brain used for intuitive business decisions and what yogis call the Third Eye. The latest research details how this area of the brain helps you contemplate both the present and the future. This is also where the brain ascertains if trust is present or not. I'm living proof.

It all works in an amazing way. The latest neuroscience now shows how from up to three metres away, you can sense if another person can be trusted, even if you've never met them.

Within a few hundredths (.07) of a second, your heart knows if you're being judged, rejected or getting a hint if the emotional space is safe. The result determines which parts of your brain engage in the conversation. Will the gates stay closed so that only your fight-or-flight process is in play, or is it safe to open the doorways to the creative parts of your brain? This is how musicians perform together.

When you meet someone who holds similar values, you sense a congruence, and your brain creates a flow of oxytocin, otherwise known as the feel-good hormone, that underpins of the relationship, whether its friendship or business. Playing music or enjoying dance, yoga or sports together also produces oxytocin.

Your first experience with it could have been as a newborn being breastfed, held and cuddled by your mother. The oxytocin cocktail is associated with a primal desire for touch and being nurtured that also activates the lymphatic and immune system.

How can leaders consistently deliver outstanding results?

What distinguishes great musicians, artists and leaders that drive them to deliver consistent, outstanding results? Why is it apparently so easy for them to reach those windows of enlightenment and moments of inspiration? How are they able to carry people into their vision for the future?

This is what I call *flow* and what athletes call *the zone*. How this capacity is developed and experienced may be different for everyone, but I believe there are some universal, creative wellsprings that trigger the oxytocin in ways that can yield tremendous results in terms of spiritual insights, scientific discoveries, artistic achievements and even material wealth.

As Buddha said, "Life brings pain, suffering is optional." *The Virtuoso Factor* is a formula for success that's grounded in psychology and simple daily rituals based on my life lessons as a mountaineer, performer and entrepreneur.

When you understand and take control of the creative elements of your life, it's possible to make dramatic shifts that will help you achieve your targets and enjoy quality time, financial freedom and a vibrant lifestyle. The greater your awareness, the easier it is to plan and design your life with grace and ease. György Seböks, an amazing musician and teacher, would often say, "Create excitement, don't get excited."

What are the five magic ego pills?

The ego is masterful and can disguise itself as any number of convincing attributes, such as personal growth, modesty or spiritual awareness and generosity. There are, however, at least five things it can't do:

- Surrender

Embracing fear as an ally is the secret. In a quantum world there's no predictability, only probability. Pretending that everything is fine prevents you from being able to welcome the unpredictable and the unknown. You can acknowledge your fears without being dominated by them. The excitement of the big win lies in the stretch beyond your comfort zone.

Performers learn to make decisions that aren't fear-based. As the adrenaline hits your system your eyes dilate, and you see better. You hear in greater detail, and you're stronger and empowered with more energy. Surrendering to the moment allows you to make use of this natural gift.

- Forgive

I've rarely heard an artist express satisfaction with a concert, and few can openly share their wins or losses. Some players immediately analyse their faults, as if to take back control of themselves and the concert. Some criticise the concert, hoping others will contradict them and help them feel more peaceful. Learning to celebrate or acknowledge your wins each day, and shifting from judgment to appreciating life's lessons, creates the space for greater connection and resonance.

Martha Graham said, "No artist is pleased. [There is] no satisfaction whatever at any time. There is only a queer divine dissatisfaction, a blessed unrest that keeps us marching and makes us more alive than the others."

- Ask for help

Are you stuck in a crevasse in life? Trainers and coaches empower you to push well past your boundaries, and beyond, with respect, care and ruthless integrity. But it's still you who smashes the goal.

- Have the ability to see the humour in all situations

    Some years ago when I was teaching at Indiana University, a senior professor looked up at all of us from his violin and said, "I find it so hard to teach and perform. In the morning I pretend I am God, and in the evening at the concert, I prove I am not."

- Accept or share unconditional love

    True connection comes when you embrace all of who you are, to make peace with your emotions and all situations. The key is to lead with authenticity and acknowledge your own depths, shadow values and positive values. Failure is a given, and it's part of showing up to truly expand who you are and live in the present.

    Why is this so vital? A flaw you see in someone else is usually a mirror of a disowned part of your self-worth. As you judge others, you're reinforcing the rejection of that part of yourself. Looking at both sides of the equation at the same time, and still accepting yourself and others, brings about a transparent connection.

What's the difference between instinct and intuition?

My entire life has been graced with music, dance, theatre and creative artistry. Sound touches me deeply, with an intensity that takes courage to explore. Performing can be fearful and sometimes unpleasant. It's as if you step into an invisible world, an eternally timeless space. The real challenge is to step past the safe and into your inner emotional landscape, so you can relax. By expanding awareness or mindset, great leaders, doctors, scientists and performers consistently access that greater consciousness.

When in flow, energy makes it almost effortless to perform at your highest standards. It's timeless and easy to respond playfully to surprises without undue stress. When you're not in this flow, everything is delivered with effort and worry. The more you experience, the more resilient and creative you become as you learn to enjoy your brilliance.

Think about how you learned to catch and throw a ball. You didn't stop to think about which muscle would be used, what speed you needed to reach a target or how much arm swing was needed. Pre-conscious thinking, or programming, took over, and it's generally more accurate and quicker than conscious processing. This pre-conscious thinking is how you drive a car, dance, and play sports and musical instruments.

Great performers first imagine the result they want and find a way to achieve that vision. Seeing the result you want to achieve sends messages to your body that intuitively carries out what's required. It's the same in business.

When performing it can feel uneasy, because intuition isn't always rational, and of course anything can happen. Staying in the safety net gives you the illusion of control to make you feel more at ease but rarely delivers the successful concert.

Peak performance demands the courage to cross the line and allow the situation to make use of you. A key is learning to surrender your attachment to how you think events should unfold.

I recall playing the Schubert Octet with the Guarneri quartet and the Lincoln Center Chamber Music Society. We were on tour across the U.S., playing a dozen concerts. The violinist had an idea about how the musical climax should be played. The cellist agreed about the emotional timing and importance, but he had an entirely different idea about how we could achieve the same brilliance. They were in full agreement on what and why but completely disagreed about how.

Night after night, we played it differently. Despite plenty of rehearsal, no one really knew what would happen. In the moment, one intention would prevail and the group would be completely synergised. The danger was electrifying, requiring each of us to surrender and be fully present and agile. It was absolutely fantastic.

The point here is that no one was focused on their bowing technique. Rather, a group of fearless musicians who trusted each other surrendered to the flow of a performance.

Here are quotations from two very different men, each brilliant in his field:

> "I believe in intuition and inspiration. ...Imagination is more important than knowledge. For knowledge is limited, whereas imagination embraces the entire world, stimulating progress, giving birth to evolution. It is, strictly speaking, a real factor in scientific research."
> ~Albert Einstein

> "I fear not the man who has practiced 10,000 kicks once, but I fear the man who has practiced one kick 10,000 times."
> ~Bruce Lee

The life of a musician appears glamorous and playful. However, the reality is that the physical stamina, emotional acumen, and intellectual curiosity required are monumental. There's no simple path to paradise. Your only comfort zone comes from how practice enhances your memory and mind by wiring your neural pathways for greater speed and accuracy. You will know frustration, fatigue, and small deaths with each downfall. This is why repetition is perhaps the single most potent force you have to improve your performance. Practice can earn you the right to feel confident.

How do you integrate playtime and success?

Incorporating playfulness into life leads to a balanced whole, and this may be why you learn best when you're having fun. The need for fun is often forgotten. Laughter stops you from taking everything too seriously and allows you to remain a little detached. This is a huge advantage when learning and performing. Fun facilitates learning and success as you're *being* rather than *doing*.

How do people measure their success?

For some, it's measured by whether they have their ideal job or make a huge amount of money. For others, it's whether their kids are healthy and prosperous, they've changed the world or they're in a long-term relationship. Fulfilment comes in a unique form to everyone, and a life may have several chapters that tell different stories.

Utopia is difficult to achieve, particularly if everyone has to agree on what utopia is. People can't even agree on which toothpaste is the best, let alone a way of living. One person's heaven is another's torture.

That being said, a successful life often involves daring to probe deeply into your self and connect with others to create something unique. To get there, stepping out of your comfort zone is almost always frightening *and* necessary.

What do you have to say to those who are wondering if they've done everything they're here to do?

That question I faced in what could have been the last few seconds of my life, is one I think most of people will have to answer, sooner or later. I don't believe there's any such thing as a self-made success. If you can't do it yourself, always figure out who you can go to for assistance. Almost every thought leader in history has had a mentor or coach who ploughed the ground to make way for their success.

Aristotle had Plato, who had Socrates. Warren Buffett had Benjamin Graham. Steve Jobs had Andy Grove of Intel. Oprah Winfrey had Maya Angelou. Carl Jung had Sigmund Freud. And Amelia Earhart had Anita Snook. In other words, behind every successful person is another successful person. And so on.

Today's CEO is no different. Business leaders are just like the world's finest conductors whose leadership transform and take people beyond the crevasses in life. They know the result can only be as strong as the talent of each member of the team. Their vision influences the culture and amplifies the experience. At the heart of it all, a judicious guiding hand encourages the individual performers to execute each movement with *clarity, confidence and courage.*

 To discover more about how Kim can help you *Elevate Your Success*, visit www.elevate-books.com/success

Nathan Bailey

Inspired Income

Nathan Bailey is an award-winning leader and entrepreneur with a passion for helping people to find and live their ideal life. Nathan has set up several centres for innovation, is a leading national and international speaker, and a recognised researcher in education and technology innovation.

He is regularly consulted for his expertise in transformational, leading-edge projects that change the way people think and work. Nathan has delivered world-first projects and has been interviewed for national radio broadcasts, television and newspapers.

The greatest joy for Nathan over the last twenty years has been his work in developing people into capable influencers and leaders and helping them find and achieve their biggest dreams and ideals.

Nathan Bailey

Inspired Income

How did you first learn about the concept of Inspired Income?

I've always wanted my life to make a difference. My dad was a leader in a non-profit, and my brother and I would help out. I was inspired to see how our little "kid helper" efforts could make such a huge difference in other people's lives.

As I started my first degree-based job, I kept seeing opportunities to make a difference, as well as colleagues who didn't realise how powerful they could be.

My team was in a bit of disarray. We were working in a new area of technology, and there wasn't a definitive leadership structure. We needed more specific priorities. After my peers and I developed a plan, a senior manager reviewed and approved it, and our team was delighted. We thrived on the clearer direction and quickly developed momentum.

It seemed pretty natural and normal for me at the time to see how I could make a difference.

I enjoyed managing and continued to rise up the ranks to more senior positions, but I became too busy. I was still making a difference, but it had become lopsided. It was all about work. I wanted more time to enjoy life, spend time with friends, be creative and explore personal projects. I wanted to make a difference outside of work.

And it wasn't just having more free time. I wanted income that would allow me to live a greater life with more health, energy and friendships.

Inspired Income

I started to explore alternative income streams and soon realised there were lots of ways to make money, but some of them were just trading one job for another. Then I discovered how I could turn my passions into profit, live my ideal day with the friendships and freedoms I wanted, and do my ideal work while earning more doing it. Of course, it's not really work when you love what you're doing.

I immediately started to make changes towards my ideal lifestyle, and then noticed there were other people who were similarly stuck. At parties, events and hanging out with friends, I would help people design their ideal lifestyle. So now, part of my inspired income is helping other people discover theirs.

Isn't Inspired Income just the same as being wealthy?

Not quite. Wealth is important, because it gives you more space in your life for new opportunities and greater meaning. It also gives you greater capacity to help others. But when you think of wealth, how much money are you thinking of? If you just want to be rich, then by earning minimum wage in Australia, you're already in the top four percent of the world's wealthiest. If you're like many Aussies, you're earning over $65,000, making you one of the hundred-million most wealthy people in the world.

If you don't *feel* wealthy, it's because you're comparing yourself, and your lifestyle, to people with more money than you have, and unless you're Bill Gates, this will always be the case.

What lifestyle would you choose if you were wealthy? Would you retire to a nice beachside villa in a sunny part of the world? Hire people to look after your house, make your meals and run errands for you? Spend most of your time relaxing with your family?

If that's your ideal lifestyle, and you're happy to live in Southeast Asia or South America, you could achieve freedom with just $25,000 a year.

There are lots of ways to generate this income, and many will require only a small portion of your time.

> **Tip 1:** Change your thinking about wealth and freedom by being specific about how you want to live your life. You'll be surprised how your feelings about income and possessions will change.

The real obstacle to wealth is not money but specificity. If you can be specific about your ideal lifestyle, then you can start having some of it *right now* and most of it within just a few years.

How does Inspired Income differ from the traditional definition of success?

You might think of success as fame and fortune. Being able to do whatever you want and attracting the respect and adoration of others. Don't be fooled by the supermarket magazines and the pictures of glamour, travel and toys. They won't bring you the great meaning and fulfilment you desire.

Lots of people would love to get rich quick, but have you ever read the story of someone who became wealthy before the age of thirty and retired? It typically goes like this:

1. Learn voraciously and look for opportunities.

2. Find an opportunity and pursue it aggressively.

3. Be wildly successful but busy.

4. Sell the business, and get lots of money and free time.

5. Buy lots of toys but get bored, because friends still have jobs and can't participate.

6. Find a more meaningful life purpose, usually education or philanthropy.

Do you want to wait to live your life with purpose and freedom, or would you like to skip a few steps? Inspired Income focuses on maximising freedom over your money, time, relationships, activity and location.

Once you switch from asking, "How much money do I have?" to "How much freedom do I have?" your priorities about money will change. You will see ways to achieve the wealth you need to live your ideal lifestyle and how you can choose to be happy and successful. You will discover how to live a meaningful life with rich relationships and great impact.

Take the time to clearly define your picture of freedom, and you will quickly be on the path to living your ideal lifestyle.

How does a person design their ideal lifestyle?

Your ideal lifestyle is made up of three parts:

- **Your ideal day**:
  Your relationships, regular activities and environment
- **Your ideal role**:
  The contribution you want to make to the world
- **Your ideal income**:
  Your source of financial independence

Most of the people I've worked with have some idea of their passion and strengths but haven't applied a structured approach to improving their life. They have dreams but haven't translated them into a daily experience they can start working towards right now.

Inspired Income is a structured model to help you achieve your ideal lifestyle. The key to its success is in the power of specificity. In the same way I did, once you define what you want, you'll realise you already have access to much of it. Specificity provides clarity, and that clarity helps you choose the most effective course of action. If you work through the model below and apply the special acceleration techniques in this chapter, you could achieve your ideal lifestyle in just a few years.

Through the seasons in your life your priorities will change, and as you achieve some parts you may find they aren't what you wanted after all. You want to keep reviewing and refining your picture of the future to ensure you can harness the power of specificity and most effectively apply the accelerators.

Where should someone start when designing their ideal lifestyle?

The best sequence is to design your ideal day, then your ideal income and ideal work. Start with your ideal day, because it's concrete and tangible. You may already have a sense of what it might be like. This is probably the area where you'll see the quickest gains towards your ideal lifestyle.

Let's begin.

Give yourself time and space. Let your imagination run free. Don't limit yourself by what you think your current reality is or how you think you *should* live.

Start to dream about your ideal day. This is not just a single magical day you only get to live once. What would a typical weekday look like if you got to choose everything about it? Consider it from start to finish, including the people, experiences, locations and outcomes you would like to be part of your regular daily routine.

> **Tip 2:** Write down your answers. You're 44% more likely to achieve your goals when you continue to review them regularly.

Here are some questions to help you get there:

- **What time do you wake up?**

    Where would you be? What kind of house, in what kind of location? Who would live there with you?

    What activities would you include in your morning routine? Consider details like nutrition, exercise, meditation and prayer. Would you develop a plan for what you want to accomplish or let the day run free?

- **If you want to work, create or explore outside your home, where would you go?**

    What form of transport would you take to get there?

- **What would your morning look like?**

    Would you spend your time being creative, planning, learning or teaching? What kind of people would you spend time with? If you're working with clients, what are they like?

    Are you working at all? You might time-box your income-generating activities by checking in one day a week on your Ebay business or spending an hour a day writing blogs and ebooks. Or perhaps you want to spend the whole day teaching people how to surf. If you had complete freedom, what would give you the most meaning and joy?

- **What would your afternoon look like?**

    Where would you have lunch? Who would join you?

    Would your afternoon include brainstorming, coaching or volunteering? Exploring nature and relaxing with the family?

- **What would you do in the early evening?**

    What activities would you enjoy doing between finishing your afternoon activities and having dinner? Consider activities like exercising, family time, community activities or a hobby.

- **What does your dinnertime look like?**

    What kind of dinner would you enjoy? Who would make it, where would you eat it and who would you eat it with?

- **What are your late evening activities?**

    What kind of activities would you enjoy prior to going to bed? This could include family time, reading, playing games or watching movies.

- **What does your bedtime look like?**

    What time would you go to bed? What kind of bed would you sleep in?

Well done. You've designed a specific future you'll enjoy and find fulfilling.

Now, here's the exciting part. Look back over your ideal day. How many of the items can you make happen right now? If you're like I am, you might say a third of them. You just haven't made them daily habits yet, because you didn't realise you wanted or could have them.

By *planning* your ideal day, you've already positioned yourself to enjoy a significant part of it straight away.

You'll start to see that further parts of your ideal day are easily achievable with some small changes. When I first did this exercise, I realised I wanted to walk to work and have an office near a café in which I could meet with clients and friends. The next day, my business partner and I inspected an office that met these criteria. I'm still enjoying the benefits of that decision, as I sit in that office and write this chapter. Imagine if you were already living more than half of your ideal day within just a few months.

The last parts of your ideal day may require you to change your work role (ideal work) or create more financial independence (ideal income).

What if someone's ideal day won't generate sufficient income?

As you focus more on the freedom of your ideal lifestyle, your income will become less important, but you'll still need money. I define financial freedom as "when you no longer need to work to live." All of your living expenses are covered by the income from your investments.

There are three key paths to achieving financial freedom:

▶ **Less costs**

   Every dollar you save in expenses pays you twice, by reducing living expenses and increasing savings.

▶ **More income**

   Develop additional sources of income that can eventually replace your salary.

- **More financial growth**

    Increase the value of what you own, so it generates more income or can be sold to invest in income-producing assets.

Which key is most important? Many people focus on reducing costs. They carry out tasks they could otherwise pay someone to do. But that's *less* freedom. Wealthy people realise time is their most scarce resource, so they look for ways to increase their income in the short term and invest as much as they can in longer-term financial growth.

The best kind of income is when people pay you to do what you love. You want to design an income stream that aligns with your ideal day and ideal work. Everyone feels busy, but time diary research shows that most people have over thirty hours of discretionary time each week. That's enough for another job. You can use that time to generate income from your passions.

Internet businesses have almost no setup costs, low running costs and can generate significant income. A well-run internet business can generate millions of dollars with a small team. While internet entrepreneurs still work hard, they work on what they're passionate about. Pat Flynn was so excited to make $7,000 in his first month online, that he started providing detailed, monthly income reports showing his journey to now earning more than $100,000 per month. See http://www.smartpassiveincome.com/my-income-reports/ for more details.

Developing an effective internet business requires significant commitment. The internet is littered with people who started a blog and stopped after three or four posts, not realising that most bloggers don't see significant income until eighteen months or more of consistent blogging.

But there's a secret to generating a great income online: you need to build a base of raving fans. Every person on a mailing list is worth one dollar per annum. If you want to generate $65,000 per annum, build a list with 65,000 subscribers and find ways to keep giving them value.

You need to find a topic you're passionate about and bring your unique perspective to it. What do you enjoy, and how can your background and experience help you explore your topic differently? Start creating content such as newsletters, blog posts, podcasts, webinars and videos that share your passion and expertise. Over time, as you deliver value, people will tune in. You can generate an income from the products you develop or by referring them to related products that provide a commission.

> **Tip 3:** Begin increasing your income through an online business on a topic you're passionate about. Your local library is a wonderful source for self-education and can provide help and computers to get you going.

With your ideal income on the way, it's time to explore your ideal work, so you can bring all three parts together into your ideal lifestyle.

What if someone isn't sure what their ideal work is? How can they find out?

We all start out as dreamers. Unfortunately, something happens between childhood aspirations and becoming an adult. At some point you learnt to *be realistic* about your future and choose a *practical* job that will cover your many life expenses.

What does the best possible job look like to you? What's a pressing problem you want to be a part of solving?

Here are some questions to help you connect with what you really enjoy doing (*write down your answers*):

- What dreams did you have as a child?
- What sparks your imagination now?
- What injustices do you see in the world that need to be addressed?
- What are you passionate about?
- What makes you angry?
- What makes you excited?
- Do you have a far-off dream job you'd like to do, but you're not sure it's possible?

As you answer these questions, you will get a sense of what you really enjoy doing and how your work could change to better align with your dreams.

If you don't know your ideal role yet, that's okay. Some people discover it as they go along. They move into a new role, master it and then grow into another one. But it's important to be clear about what you enjoy doing. Opportunity and money are attracted to certainty. When you're clear about what you want, it's more likely to come to you.

If you still find this challenging, get a coach to help you. With a little guidance, most people can make good progress in a single session.

You might also want to explore these questions:

- What kind of problems do you enjoy solving? What kinds of work garners you the most compliments? Your greatest contributions will be where your strengths and passions overlap.
- Is there a common thread in the stories of successful people you admire that resonates with you?

- What problems seem easy to you that other people find difficult?
- In the last year, when have you had a satisfying day? What happened? What made it so satisfying? What kind of role would provide that kind of satisfaction on a daily basis?

By now you should be feeling a little excitement. Just by describing your ideal lifestyle in specific terms you can start to see it, as well as some immediate steps you can take towards it. But if you're struggling, then you may need to spend more time cultivating your dream in order to overcome your internal resistance.

> **Tip 4:** Once you're clearer about your ideal role, work out the smaller steps for positioning yourself into it, perhaps as a volunteer or via your online business. Keep your list of steps somewhere prominent, and review them daily. Celebrate growth in your life as you achieve each step.

How does someone overcome obstacles on the path to their ideal lifestyle?

In the quest for your ideal lifestyle dream, you're going to face resistance from yourself and others. You might feel like your dream is too hard, it won't work, or that you don't have enough time, money or other resources to do it. Instead of looking at what you can't do, identify the steps you *can* do, and start with them. You will build momentum and confidence in yourself, and the challenges that had seemed insurmountable will look smaller and easier to tackle.

Your friends and family might find your ideal lifestyle hard to believe. Remember, dreaming big isn't normal. People like the comfortable and familiar.

Your dream needs to be cultivated. Like a newly planted seed, it needs plenty of optimistic sunshine and the pulling of the occasional weed of distraction or discouragement.

Nelson Mandela's big dream took decades to cultivate. He read, wrote and talked with others. But above all else, he continued to believe in his dream. Who would imagine that a man inside a prison cell would prove more powerful than the leader of his country? Mandela's dream was so well cultivated that it continues to impact South Africa years after his death.

Here are some great ways to cultivate your dream:

- Spend time with people who've achieved similar dreams. You want your thinking to be shaped by those who not only believe it can be done but have done it.

- Find a podcast, YouTube channel or TED talk category that feeds your dream. Watch or listen to one episode each day. You need to saturate yourself with new ways of thinking about your ideal lifestyle.

- Find someone who has skills or expertise that could contribute to your ideal lifestyle. Spend time with those who speak into your dream.

- Visualise your ideal lifestyle. This is how Olympians prepare for winning the gold when they've never had the experience. Imagine each step of the process in as realistic detail as possible, including the sights, senses and steps. Visualisation makes the experience more real and familiar, thus making it much easier to achieve.

> **Tip 5:** Visualise your dream daily, and feed it by spending time with likeminded people and on self-education.

How can someone become more action-oriented?

Many of the people I've coached are in their first or second job. They have technical skills in their field but are still learning how to do great work as part of a team. I help them learn how to start quickly and keep moving.

Your ideal lifestyle needs the same momentum. Get comfortable with imperfect starts, or you'll spend your life waiting for a perfect future that will never come. Here are some ways to take action quickly:

- **Adopt the two second rule**

    When you think of an action that will move you forward, and you can do it now, start it within two seconds. This will get you acting before your logical mind can generate all of the reasons why you shouldn't. Every action you take helps build momentum, which increases your desire and reduces resistance.

- **Break it down**

    If a task seems a little daunting, break it down into smaller tasks you can tackle or seek some help. You might discover your thinking is being limited by your previous experience.

- **Do a productive activity every day**

    Have you ever worked with a team of people with similar skills and experience, and yet one person seemed to achieve far more than anyone else? They've discovered the power of consistency. Take action *every* day.

> **Tip 6:** Learn the value of momentum by getting comfortable with imperfect starts and taking action every day.

When struggling with difficult actions, remember that willpower is like a muscle. It grows by making great decisions but gets fatigued with use throughout the day. Tackle your most difficult tasks in the morning and combine them with an activity you enjoy doing. This can help to develop a positive association with the tough task in the future, so it's easier to do. Every time you successfully complete the task, you'll reinforce that positive association.

How can someone find the next action that will make the biggest difference?

Not all tasks are created equal. Some will accelerate all of the others. Identifying these lynchpin tasks can hugely affect how much you get done.

> **Tip 7:** Approximately 20% of your effort is responsible for 80% of your outcomes, so learn where to invest your efforts for the greatest impact.

If you reflect back on your day at work, you can probably think of a couple of high-impact actions. The Pareto principle recognises this gap between outcome and effort. Most sales come from a few big customers, a majority of complaints come from a few people and the main source of your profits comes from a few products. Imagine if your whole workday could be as productive as your highest impact actions.

Ask yourself these questions to help find your highest impact next action:

1. "What's the *one* thing I can do such that by doing it, everything else will be easier or unnecessary?" (Gary Keller)

2. "Instead of dealing with urgent problems, what can I do to prevent those problems?" (Stephen Covey)

3. "What would it look like if doing 'X' was easy?" (Tim Ferriss)

The most important time to apply the Pareto principle is at the start of your day. The first thirty minutes can make a huge difference to your focus and productivity. Plan out your day, and spend your first few interruption-free minutes working on your highest priority.

Make time to look ahead. You can often get future tasks moving with minimal effort by doing a small piece of preparation each day, so all of the pieces are in place when you need to deliver. Don't be afraid to politely follow up with others on a daily basis. The squeaky wheel gets the grease.

Why is it so important to maintain focus?

What you focus on, you get more of. Why? When you choose to spend time on an activity, you're telling your brain it's important. The more time you spend, the more important your brain will think it is.

As you focus on a single task, you slowly build momentum. Your subconscious explores the problem in parallel with your conscious mind, and you get creative ideas about how to do it better. You feel fully engaged and lose track of time as you enter a highly productive state known as flow. And then…bing! You get an email.

At this point, all of that momentum is dissipated. The cost of interruptions is much higher than you realise. Research shows it can take anywhere from a few minutes to a half an hour to get fully back up to speed.

Worse than that, people who multitask decrease their ability to focus. In other words, those interruptions aren't just costing you time and slowing you down, they're also weakening your decision-making muscle.

You need to redesign your physical, mental and electronic workspace to maximise productivity:

1. **Disable notifications**

    Turn off new email notifications. Add a vacation message explaining you'll be checking your email at certain times each day. Turn off notifications on your mobile phone or put it into aeroplane mode.

2. **Schedule office hours for discussions**

    Let your colleagues know that you're working on a challenging project, and you'd prefer it if they could visit you during a specific time period.

3. **Minimise distractions**

    Keep pictures of your family or any other mementos that give you warm fuzzies but remove anything that might catch your attention.

4. **Work in cycles**

    Use a method like the Pomodoro technique, which is twenty-five minutes of work with a five-minute break, to plan, measure and improve the way you do chunks of work.

5. **Programme your brain for success**

    Tell yourself future truths such as, *I'm working on X* or *Working on X is easy and fun* or *My capacity to focus is improving*. Your subconscious will want to make it true.

What about all of those activities people don't want to do or can't do?

Use the power of reciprocity. There are lots of people who are keen to help if you just know how to ask.

When you regularly go out for coffee with a friend, you'll probably have a discussion about whose turn it is to pay. If one person pays all of the time, that wouldn't seem fair. If they do something nice for you, then you feel you should do something nice in return. That's reciprocity.

Research shows that people who give help at work are more likely to succeed. Why? Because givers build up a bank of reciprocity to draw from in the future when they need a favour. The same research also shows that seventy-five to ninety percent of all giving comes through asking. Even those who are keen to help you need to know what kind of help you'd like.

Some people might even enjoy tasks you consider boring or unpleasant. It's not just about different skills and passions. Sometimes people are tired or stressed, and they want something "boring" to do to help them feel successful. When delegating tasks, if you can find out how to give someone more control, simpler execution, greater impact or greater responsibility, then you can have a win-win outcome.

By developing workflows and checklists for your routine tasks, you make it easier for someone else to take them over. You also save yourself the risk of forgetting steps. Each time you do the task, you can refine the checklist to make the outcome easier, quicker and of higher quality. Then when you do pass it on, it will be a much better task.

As you consistently deliver beyond expectations, you'll develop a reputation for success. People will want to help you out of reciprocity but also to be involved in your success. Everyone likes to back a winner. If you collaborate and deliver well, you're the winner everyone will want to back, particularly if you're generous enough to remember their contributions whenever your success is recognised.

Why is it important to measure improved performance?

When you're specific about your ideal lifestyle, you can track, analyse and improve your performance. If you get one percent better each week, you will be over a hundred and sixty times better by the end of the year. But how do you work out what to change?

Research shows that exercise can cause a fifteen percent improvement in work performance. How do you find which kind of exercise is most effective for you? Websites like Google do A/B testing. They serve up page A to half of their users and page B to the other half, and see which page gets the better response. They analyse where your mouse goes, what you click on and how long you take to determine which aspects of the page have the greatest impact. You could use A/B testing on your exercise options to find out what works best for your energy, motivation and health.

To learn more about using measures to break patterns and build momentum, read the article at www.inspiredincome.com.au/measures.

What's the first step to take?

You've already adopted an important step in personal growth, which is reading books. Because of the publication process, books tend to have higher quality information than most online materials. They also tend to have online ratings and reviews, which allows you to get the best return for your reading time.

But even with great books and other resources, at some point you're going to get stuck. When you do, the best piece of advice I can give you is to get a coach.

They can help move mountains you can't move on your own. I see coaches as a training partner, in that a problem shared is a problem halved. They're also an accelerator, because 10X growth requires 10X insight. Even though I'm a coach, I still use coaches, because I've found that:

- they make it easier to do hard tasks
- synergy with a partner accelerates progression
- their observation provides critical feedback

In areas of strength, like business, I tend to hire a coach for a defined period of time to help me achieve a specific objective. In areas of challenge, like personal fitness, I've hired a coach on an ongoing basis to help me achieve consistent growth.

How do you find a great coach? Ideally, by referral. Otherwise, read what they've written, visit their live events and talk to the people who've bought their products and services. Choose a coach who's capable, cares about their clients and is trustworthy. A good coach should be able to provide tangible help on a real-world problem from the first session.

This ideal lifestyle method sounds like a lot of work. Is the end result worth it?

Life is short. Even with the secrets I've given for getting more time, your years on earth will go by in an increasingly quick blur. In the end, when you look back on your life and evaluate it, what will you see?

Bronnie Ware is a palliative care nurse who's cared for hundreds of people during the last few weeks of their lives. She discovered the most common regrets all relate to meaning and purpose: dreams, work, feelings, friends and happiness. The number one regret was, "I wish I'd had the courage to live a life true to myself, not the life others expected of me." In her book, *The Top 5 Regrets of the Dying*, Bronnie reports that, "Most people had not honoured even half of their dreams and had to die knowing that it was due to choices they had made, or not made."

Big dreams are hard work, but they're also rewarding. Everyone has read or heard stories about people who started with the seed of an idea and went on to change the world. They're inspiring. It's exciting to experience the drama of their story as it unfolds. It resonates on a deep level, because everyone is made for greatness.

The world is facing huge challenges in areas such as inequity, environment, energy, safety, health and growth. Can you make a difference with your ideal lifestyle? Can you be part of a movement that leaves a lasting impact on the world? Make a choice to live your life in such a way that in the end, you will have no regrets.

I wish you all the best in taking the first steps towards your ideal lifestyle. I'm available to help clients who are ready for change. Remember, your life is important. Make the most of it for yourself and others.

 To discover more about how Nathan can help you *Elevate Your Success*, visit www.elevate-books.com/success

Kim Tiong

Mind Over Matchsticks

Kim is a personal transformation coach and speaker who assists her clients in awakening their true power, so they're able to say, "I am enough just as I am" and achieve their seemingly impossible goals.

Kim started her career as an external auditor, working with some of the most reputable professional services firms in the industry, until she went on a self-development journey that led her to her true calling.

Kim has been invited to speak at conferences and events by organisations such as The Chartered Accountants Australia and New Zealand (formerly the Institute of Chartered Accountants in Australia) and the Australian Institute of Management. Her mission is to enable her clients to make their internal vision a reality from a place of inspiration, creation and flow.

Kim Tiong
Mind Over Matchsticks

What's your biggest life lesson?

I used to spend so much time and money looking for the silver bullet, but ultimately the biggest lesson I've learned is to work on my internal world and my deepest wounds, shame and guilt, so I can love, value and make peace with every part of me and be empowered.

What I experience is a direct reflection of my internal world. I'm responsible for creating my experiences and results in life. They're based on my actions, the stories I tell myself, my coping mechanisms and strategies, as well as my conscious and unconscious beliefs, emotional addictions and wounds. Nothing has meaning except the meaning I give it.

That's what my workshops, retreats and coaching all focus on: empowering others by owning who you are. I'm not talking about power in the forceful, pushy way it's sometimes used but instead as a beautiful inward journey of awakening your *personal* power.

As tempting as it can be to blame others and play the victim, I know if someone triggers me, it isn't them or the situation. It's about my unhealed emotional pain. Everyone has a choice. I can choose to let it affect me or let it go. I've come to embrace the triggers and the challenges, because they point towards what I still need to work on inside of myself. They represent opportunities to learn even more about my internal world and be even more empowered.

So, here's an opportunity for you to take a bit of an inward journey, if you'd like to come along for the ride:

Think of something, or someone, who irritates, aggravates, frustrates or annoys you. Really get specific about what it is that gets to you.

For example, perhaps you're irritated when someone continuously taps their fingers on the table, in which case I would ask what it is about this gesture that really irritates you. Is it that they don't respect other people's sense of space, or are they disturbing your peace and quiet?

Another example could be when people try to take control of a situation. Again, you may need to get more specific about this. For example, is it because when they take control it means you don't get to express your point of view, or does it stifle your freedom?

Ask yourself, *How do I try to take control in my own life?* It doesn't have to be the exact same situation. Think about whether you take control in your work life or with friends and family. Maybe you take control on a personal level around your health, spirituality, finances or emotions.

If you look closely at what you're triggered by, you'll begin to understand it's about you or some part of yourself you don't like.

An example of a reflection might be that you try to control your emotions and hence stifle your ability to express what's really going on for you that might annoy and frustrate you. Or it could be that you're controlling in relationships, which you may feel a bit guilty about.

The point of this exercise isn't to name and shame. It's just an opportunity to get to know and make peace with another part of yourself. Try to understand the reason behind what annoys you, and sit with any emotion that comes up without trying to change it. Just breathe through it until you feel it release and let go. Then ask yourself what you can do about this trait, so you can give yourself peace.

When you come to accept that part of yourself, this particular behaviour in other people won't irritate you anymore.

This exercise can sometimes be challenging and a little confronting, so if you stayed with me and completed it, you did an awesome job. Give yourself a high five and know I'm mentally and energetically giving you a high five back.

If you were speaking to your younger self, what advice would you give?

Trust yourself and your intuition. You may think other people know better than you, but just because they speak louder or with more conviction, doesn't mean that they know what's best for *you*.

Forget the shoulds and trying to fit into someone else's idea of perfection. You know exactly what's right for you, so trust yourself and take one step in that direction. Just like when you were hiking the Inca Trail, put one foot in front of the other.

I love you, and you're enough just as you are. Trying to find that validation externally is a waste of time, because you already have it, and it's not what you're looking for. What you're looking for is *you* to love yourself just as you are.

When you hear this, part of you will think, *What a load of crap*, and I wouldn't change anything for you or try to convince you otherwise. Everything you're going through, as challenging as it may seem, helps you become the amazing person you are today in ways you can't even imagine, and your journey will lead you to these realisations anyway, it's just about getting there in your own time.

Have you had any aha moments that changed everything for you?

Two come to mind. I started my career in a corporate role, and while I was performing well and on the outside my life looked perfect, on the inside I was miserable, both at work and at home in my marriage. One day I woke up and asked myself, *If I died tomorrow, would I be happy with my life?* and realised I would be frustrated and sad that I'd wasted my short time in this world living my life according to other people's expectations and not being true to myself. That started me on my personal development journey, which gave me the courage to leave my job and marriage and set off to create a life that was true to me. It was the moment that started me on my current trajectory.

The other *aha* moment that stands out was realising a lot of what I was experiencing in life came down to how much I loved and valued myself. When I could drop the mask, be vulnerable and okay with certain parts of myself I was ashamed and guilty about, I got to a place where I could say, "This is me. I have nothing to prove," and my life started to flow.

What personal decisions have made a difference in your life?

Every decision where I followed my heart rather than the *should* has turned out to be the right one for me. The big decisions that stand out are:

- leaving my corporate career to set up my first business
- leaving my husband and moving to Sydney to set up my life coaching business
- choosing to take time out to focus on myself and my wellbeing by doing deep inner work, changing my mindset, and embracing spirituality rather than my career

These decisions all made a hugely positive difference in my life. I wouldn't be where I am now, both personally and professionally, if I hadn't made them.

Conversely, the ones I've made based on the shoulds or other people's expectations, or at least my perception of their expectations, have provided many of my difficulties, a lot of the pain and some big learning experiences.

What are some of the common barriers stopping people from living their lives?

I think a lot comes down to not loving and valuing yourself. I don't only mean this in the, *Can you look in the mirror and love what you see?* kind of way, but also in the *Can you drop the mask, be real and still be okay?* kind of way. I think these are the common barriers:

- Not believing in yourself and letting various fears get in the way of taking action towards your goals, such as fear of what other people may think, fear of failing or succeeding, fear of the unknown and fear of a potential change in a living situation.

- Your mindset, including the stories you tell yourself and the labels you give yourself, like "I'm not the type of person who…" or "I'm too (old/young/smart/dumb) to…" or "xxx doesn't work for me, because…" or "I'm not (clever/good/connected) enough to…" These stories and labels become the walls of the box within which you get yourself stuck.

- Wanting confidence and certainty or for everything to be perfect before starting a new venture.

    Confidence and certainty come along the way and grow with the more actions you take. Your brain initially tries to keep you safe by projecting reasons and rationalisations for why you shouldn't take action, but if you take small steps in a new direction, your brain realises it's not that bad and says, *We didn't die after all. Maybe this is okay* and will start doing it more.

- Not being aware of strategies you often unconsciously resort to that can keep you stuck in old patterns.

    Some call it self-sabotage, but I think it pertains to strategies that help you through a particular time, and since it worked for you in that situation, you continue to use that strategy throughout your life, unless you take steps to change it. Your brain doesn't understand the difference between a good and bad strategy. All it knows is that if it didn't kill you, keep doing it.

What helped you achieve your current success is the very thing preventing you from moving forward.

For example, someone who's a superstar performer may get promoted to the next level because of their ability, but just because they're good at doing their job doesn't necessarily mean they will be an amazing manager or business owner who can step back and trust others to get the job done. Instead of asking yourself what you need to do differently, you keep doing the same thing expecting a different result. This is often quoted as being the definition of insanity.

- Not trusting your own judgement and not listening to and honouring yourself but instead trying to please everyone else. This may not prevent you from taking action but from taking action in the right direction.

What's the best way to help people overcome these barriers?

Through my coaching, retreats and workshops, I help people uncover and make peace with those parts of themselves they would rather forget. The purpose is not to have a name-and-shame party but to gain love and acceptance by loving and accepting yourself and owning your personal power. When you shine a light in the dark places, you realise the situation isn't that bad after all.

The more inner work you do, the more you start to understand yourself, your stories and patterns, and your coping mechanisms and strategies. The more you own the different parts of yourself, the more empowered you can become.

You also start to realise it's not just you who's feeling alone/not enough/unsafe/unloved. Many experience similar wounds in their own way, it's just that no one talks about it, because they feel ashamed or guilty or embarrassed and scared of judgment.

It may sound a little strange, but stay with me. If you like, you can start by doing this mirror exercise. Look in the mirror, acknowledge and accept whatever comes up and keep breathing and sending yourself love. Think of the you in the mirror as another person who's only looking for someone to hear them.

Then complete the following sentence stem with the first thing that comes to mind:

"Something I don't want you to know about me is..."

Keep breathing as you continue to look at yourself while acknowledging what you've just said. Think of any judgments or negative voices that come up as being like a child that keeps trying to get your attention. Acknowledge them and let them go off and do their own thing. Don't interact but just observe them.

Sit with any emotions that may come up. Don't try to change them, just stay with them until they've run their course. Acknowledge what you've just been brave enough to admit to yourself. Really look into your own eyes and spend a couple of minutes sending love and appreciation to yourself, whether it's by telling yourself *I love you* or imagining sending energy to yourself. It may sound a little odd, but it can have a powerful impact on your life.

What do you think inspires people?

The feeling that you're developing and evolving personally and making a difference in the world. I think this tends to fall in line with finding your life purpose. That thing that lights you up inside and makes you feel alive.

Generally, people who are on purpose have overcome a big challenge in their life and then feel inspired to help others do the same. This incorporates giving back and a sense of fulfilment. It's also a constant source of inspiration, because when you help heal others you're also healing yourself, which means you develop and evolve.

I think a lot of external achievements like the big house, the fancy car and having a lot of money, may be aspirational but not necessarily inspirational. It's often mistakenly thought these material possessions will make you happy and fulfilled and at last gain you the love and acceptance you seek. It may seem to drive you for a time, but it's actually a desperate need to feel okay and enough by acquiring more possessions, rather than a true inspiration.

If you're not inspired, you need external motivation to get through the day and do what you need to do, but when you find your purpose and are courageous enough to go in that direction, you're truly inspired, and it's almost like an internal drive or a pull to go forward.

What's your most inspiring client story?

One of my beautiful clients is a PhD student who wants to be the Australian expert in her particular field. Since we've been working together she was invited to attend a conference in Japan where she met high-ranking Australian officials and industry leaders from around the world. She presented three of her papers at a conference in South Africa, and as I write this, she recently came back from attending a World Health Organisation conference and United Nations Conference where she spoke of her ideas for a new model for the industry.

She did all of this while working part-time helping her husband run their family businesses, being a mother and completing her PhD.

The people I work with don't need a coach. They're incredible, inspiring and amazing people in their own right. They're not the loudest, biggest, boldest or brashest, but they're wonderful people who are just doing what inspires them and are out to make a difference in the world.

They choose me as their coach, because they know the journey to the top can at times be lonely, and it's nice to have a safe space to openly reflect and share their deepest desires and fears, while also being reminded of how extraordinary they are when they temporarily lose sight of that fact. But ultimately, they don't need me. They choose me, which is a real honour.

How can someone find their life purpose?

I first heard this from Benjamin J Harvey, so the credit goes to him. I love the idea of *un-transmuted grandiosity*. What this means is that if you can create a business or career out of your biggest shame, you will always be inspired to do what you do, because you will always be inspired to heal yourself.

Also know that your purpose can change, so while you may start taking steps in one direction, like being lost in a desert, you can course correct as you go along and are not tied to any particular outcome. This has happened to me. While I may start in one area with my coaching, as I grow, develop and heal different parts of myself, my business and focus changes with time. Life is fluid, because you're constantly changing and developing, and I think that's a beautiful thing.

Do you live your love?

Absolutely. And having spent so many years not living my love, I know this is the only way I will ever choose to live.

How did you decide on the name 134 Matchsticks for your business?

It's based on the idea that while you're bombarded by millions of bits of information every second, according to NLP research, you can only consciously process about 134 bits. So it's like millions of matchsticks falling on your head each second, and you can only grab a handful. What you grab creates your perception of reality and influences your mindset in that moment, which emphasises that you're essentially responsible for your life experiences.

Why is mindset important?

Because your mindset shapes and creates your experiences and determines your results in life. Everything experienced is a reflection of what's going on internally.

You can't consciously process everything going on around you at any point in time, so your brain filters the information through your reticular activating system (RAS), which is a set of connected nuclei in the brain of vertebrates that's responsible for regulating wakefulness and sleep-wake transitions. It's based on your beliefs, wounds, stories and experiences.

It's like wearing a special pair of glasses that lets you choose whether you focus on what you want or what you don't. This is important, because whatever you focus on, grows.

Think about elite athletes and their winning mindset. Imagine if Michael Jordan went into a game focusing on the more than nine-thousand shots he missed, the almost three-hundred games he lost and the twenty-six times he'd been trusted to take the game-winning shot and missed.

Imagine if Richard Branson was scared of failing. He would have stopped at his student magazine, or even at dropping out of school at sixteen.

Instead of seeing failure as bad and focusing on all of the mistakes made in the past, successful people credit their failures as the *reason* behind their success. They see it as the only way to learn.

You can either play the victim or take responsibility. Your mindset can hinder or empower you. Either way, you have a choice.

How does someone keep inspired on a daily basis?

The most lasting way is to find your purpose, that thing that drives you and lights you up inside, and live that every day.

Until then, set the intention or ask yourself a question that presupposes what you want. For instance, "Why is everything so inspiring today?" or "How many ways can I be inspired today?"

I think it's also about acknowledging that you can't be inspired every single moment of your life. Accept that everyone needs down-time and trust you're where you're supposed to be in each moment.

What mindset do you believe is needed in order to create a great life?

Realising how powerful you are and that you're responsible for creating what you experience in life, while also coming from a place of gratitude. I do believe this world is an amazing place and that everything happens for a reason as a way of helping you to develop and grow as a person. This belief is an empowering and beautiful place to come from.

Does visualisation actually work?

Yes and no. It depends on what's going on for you when you do it.

I've had some great successes with visualisation and manifestation, such as finding places to live, manifesting my perfect soul mate relationship and always finding free parking. These are the reasons visualisation might not work:

- You don't really trust it will happen, either because you don't trust yourself or the process, or because you otherwise get discouraged.

- You're not energetically aligned with what you're trying to manifest. If you don't really believe you deserve it, have some other limiting beliefs or are sabotaging yourself in some way, you have a needy attachment to the outcome, which sends a sign that you're lacking what you're trying to manifest and hence don't really trust it will happen.

- You expect it to happen a certain way and are not aware of the opportunities that actually do exist. It often doesn't happen the way you plan, but you can get so fixated on your vision of the way you think it will happen that you completely miss the other opportunities that present themselves.

I actually wrote a blog post regarding my thoughts on manifestation. If you're interested, head to http://134matchsticks.com.au/three-thoughts-on-manifesting/.

Do you have a coach or mentor or someone to motivate you?

All of the above. I'm a coach and absolutely believe in the power of coaching, so I definitely have my own coach.

I also believe in the power of mentors and am fortunate to have had inspiring people mentor me throughout my whole working life, both in my corporate career and with my own business. I absolutely know I wouldn't be where I am now without the guidance of these amazing people, and I'm so grateful to have them in my life.

I also know how important external influences are in helping to get to where you want to go, so I regularly catch up with people in the same, or similar, industries and on the same path, so we can all help each other and hold each other accountable to our highest potential.

How do these coaches and mentors make a difference to your success?

Some of the ways include:

- having an unbiased, non-judgmental space to voice your deepest desires and greatest fears

- having someone point out your blind spots, because most of the time you can't see your own

- not letting yourself off easy, like doing a workout by yourself as compared to working out with a personal trainer

- having someone to help you keep the bigger picture in sight, so you don't get lost in your own stories and forget the amazingly inspiring, powerful person you are, while also holding you accountable to your highest potential

What are your favourite ways to relax and keep balance in your life?

▸ Connecting with nature either through going to the beach or lake or hiking in the mountains.

▸ Being physically active through yoga, running, walking or swimming.

▸ Travelling.

▸ Spending time with the amazing people in my life.

▸ Listening to good music and dancing around my house with my family.

▸ Having me-time. I go to art galleries and get creative, even though I'm not the world's best artist.

- Doing meditation, retreats and other processes that are focused around emotional release, deep inner work and healing.

How can people be happier in life?

Realise that no one is going to give you the permission you're waiting for, so make the choice to be happier in life. Set the intention, *Today I'm going to have an amazing day,* and keep reminding yourself throughout the day. Then see how many amazing things happen.

Also take a moment to ask yourself what you enjoy doing and what has you lose track of time. Then schedule in more of those activities. This is a great way to help energise you and reconnect with yourself.

It's also good to connect with nature and the people you love.

How can people overcome fear?

Ignore those negative voices in your head, and just do it. Have that difficult conversation, call that client, take steps towards changing careers or create that vision in your head. Don't wait for the confidence and certainty, and don't wait for everything to be perfect. It likely never will be, at least not in your own mind.

Think about the new experiences you've attempted in your life like starting a new job or new relationship and meeting new people. Did you have the confidence you wanted? Did you have some kind of fear? It's likely you did, but you went through with it anyway.

People often try to overcome the fear and want the confidence first before trying something new. But that's not how it works. Confidence comes along the way when you start to take action. The more action you take, and the more familiar you become with that experience, the more confident you become.

Fear is just another strategy to keep you safe in your little box, because who knows what could be waiting out there to harm you? Your mind brings out all of its strategies, like distraction and procrastination, feeling overwhelmed, comfort eating, watching too much TV or whatever has worked in the past, so you can stay safe.

What's the one area of your life you've been avoiding? If you think of something and get a slight feeling of queasiness or panic, you know you're on the right track. What's your vision of the end outcome or goal? What's one small step you can take in the next day that will have you heading in that direction? Have the big vision but know you need to take a lot of small steps to achieve it.

Just act, and the confidence will come.

What's one activity someone could do now to change their life?

Ask yourself, in the words of Christie Marie Sheldon, a lofty question. This is a question that presupposes what you want. Something like, *Why is everything so easy today?* The question presupposes that everything is easy.

I do it all of the time, and it's amazing how something simple like this can change your mindset and view of the world so easily. It shows the power of the questions you ask yourself, both positive and negative.

Why do you think so many people are overwhelmed and unhappy with their life?

As palliative care nurse, Bronnie Were, writes in her book *The Top 5 Regrets of the Dying*, the most common regret is, *I wish I'd had the courage to live a life true to myself, not the life others expected of me.*

Were noted that most people had not honoured even half of their dreams and had to die knowing it was due to choices they'd made or not made.

I would take that a step further and say that many people don't live with purpose, because they're too scared to admit *to themselves* what they really, really want and to go for it. This means they get stuck in other people's judgments and expectations, as well as their own, as to how they "should" be living.

It's amazing how well you can *rationalise* an undesirable situation. It's just another way your brain tries to keep you safe and away from unfamiliar situations.

What's the best success tip you could give?

Combine deep inner work with external action in the direction of your dreams. Keep going despite the fears, negative voices, shouldn'ts and any other barrier that presents itself.

Deep inner work is for the wounds that haven't healed, what triggers you, emotional addictions, the stories you tell yourself and the strategies you use. Peel back the layers, and have the courage, patience and love to see what's there. Then start making peace with those parts of yourself you would rather forget were there.

The aim is for *you* to love and value yourself, every part of yourself, so that you can be in a space of having nothing to prove to and nothing to hide from yourself or anyone else.

Do you have an approach to your coaching?

My focus is all about empowering my clients to make their internal vision a reality, and for me there are two parts to this:

The first is that being empowered means being yourself by awakening the power within and having a deep sense of coming home.

This can involve peeling back the layers, dropping the mask and having the courage to explore what's underneath the surface. It includes revisiting old wounds, shining a light on the parts of yourself you'd rather forget, and appreciating that all of your stories, strategies, wounds, shame, guilt and fears are just protective layers you've created. They've shaped you and helped you get to where you are today.

To me, being empowered is not about having to tell the whole world your deepest fears and desires. It's more about being able to admit them to yourself and loving and accepting how they're a part of you. It means coming to a place of gratitude and appreciation.

The second is that external action involves admitting what you want in life while thanking the negative voices that tell you why you shouldn't have it and taking steps in that direction anyway. People often say they don't know what they want, but it's more likely they know exactly what they want but are too fearful, ashamed or guilty to admit it to themselves.

As Bryan Franklin says, our deepest desires are at the intersection of who we are and what we're ashamed of. You need to make friends with the fear. As Brene Brown says, fear will always be there, so you may as well invite it along for the ride. Go for what you want. It's the only way to live a fulfilling life.

To discover more about how Kim can help you *Elevate Your Success*, visit

www.elevate-books.com/success

Ivor Lok

Dreams Do Come True

IMPACT ➔ INFLUENCE ➔ TRANSFORM

Ivor Lok cares deeply about effecting change. His life purpose is to inspire individuals to break through their invisible boundaries in order to reveal their true magnificence.

After seeking change in his own life and experiencing a transformational shift of psychology, he became a licensed Bob Proctor Presenter and Peak Performance Results Coach for Tony Robbins. With over ten thousand sessions of coaching and affecting change in hundreds of individuals, Ivor is truly living his dream.

Ivor Lok

Dreams Do Come True

Live Passionately

What's your biggest life lesson?

When I was growing up I was ill mannered and a live wire. Although by nature I was quiet, I struggled to control my anger, but I was also able to flick back to calm quickly. I never thought of it as control, but rather manipulation, of the people at the receiving end of my anger.

Even though I thought I was happy, I was suffering and thinking that the whole world was against me. I was negative about life and always thought the worst of people. I suffered from road rage and put myself and my passengers at risk many a time. I'm not proud about this, and I want to apologize to anybody who has witnessed my bad behaviour.

It wasn't until I'd begun my personal development journey and after attending a Bob Proctor event, "You Were Born Rich", that I realized my current paradigm, meaning my programming, modelling and beliefs, weren't serving me, and that my past does not equal my future. I realised I needed to develop a different way of thinking.

So began the journey of attempting to have a more positive mindset. I started to change the way I viewed the world. I found it helpful to do gratitude lists every day. This assisted me in becoming much happier, and I even remember my colleagues asking why I was so happy. But somehow I still found it hard to control my anger.

I kept reading and studying as many books on human behaviour I could find and eventually found Neuro Linguistic Programming (NLP). This enhanced the control I needed to manage my anger.

It was only after attending a Tony Robbins event called "Unleash the Power Within" that I understood how to truly control my emotional state. I remember Tony taking us through different emotions as a display of how you can change your emotional state in a heartbeat.

I would say this was my biggest life lesson, and it's one I'm proud to say I've mastered. It impacted my life so much that I decided I would set a goal to become a coach for Tony Robbins. I've realized that goal, and I'm now a Peak Performance Results Coach for Robbins Research International.

LESSON

How to get into an empowered state (as learnt from Tony Robbins):

Step One: change your physiology.

Step Two: change your focus.

Step Three: change your language.

Please go to my website, ivorlok.com, to get a full description and audio that will walk you through the exact steps to get into an empowered state.

What does love mean to you?

Love is an emotion, a feeling, a state of mind you can control. When I was younger, I believed that love needed to come from somebody else. I was the youngest of four children and craved the attention. I would often act out to seek attention and love. My parents loved me immensely, and I'm so grateful my father retired when I was still in school, because I got to actively know him. I've always had love from my mother as well, completely and unconditionally.

Now that I've developed as a person, I understand love comes from within. It's having gratitude and appreciation that allows me to remain in a loving state. I'm also fortunate to have a lovely wife and two beautiful daughters who love me unconditionally. I now believe I am love, so therefore I am able to give it unconditionally.

LESSON

Each day, write down three things you're grateful for that has happened in the last twenty-four hours and see love begin to shine through you. Change your focus to what's already beautiful and working in your life.

If you were speaking to your younger self, what advice would you give?

1. Never give up!!!

2. Learn how to set goals. It's so incredibly important, and most people ignore this easy step and suffer decades of wandering around in the wilderness without direction.

3. Have the courage to go out there. Life begins at the end of your comfort zone. Don't worry about how you're going to achieve your goal. You'll figure it out if your desire is strong enough.

4. Listen to the sound of your own drum. Following someone else's will lead you away from your desires and dreams, and ultimately, your destiny.

5. Read a lot of books on successful people, as success leaves clues, and it's the easiest way to receive role modelling beyond your circumstances.

6. Live life fully by doing activities that will help you develop and grow.

7. Stay away from drugs.

8. Learn what you need, in accordance to the goals you want to accomplish. Be selective with the information you learn, as a lot of it is not in alignment with what you want and therefore is a waste of time.

9. Remember, you don't need to know how until you need to know how.

How would you like to be remembered?

I would like to be remembered for doing the best I could with the resources I had and as someone who was:

- willing to challenge the status quo and danced with the uncertainty of living outside of my comfort zone

- loving and kind to any human being and left a legacy that would impact the world, so everyone could have a way to achieve their destiny

- always striving to do better, not because I wasn't doing well, but because there's always a new level

I also want to be known as someone who knew how to have fun and suck the juice out of life but who always knew there was work to be done, because you only get one shot at living an amazing life.

What would you like your legacy be?

My legacy is to impact billions of lives that will have a ripple effect long after I'm gone.

I want to leave a self-perpetuating fund, as well as scholarships, that will be there to provide the resources for future generations to learn, grow and develop.

What's the one message you wish to share with the world?

Know thyself. This was the greatest message I received when I began to understand who I was. I can say that without having that message, I would probably still be an angry, bitter, sad, depressed person, wandering around without any direction.

What's the worst thing that's ever happened to you, and how did you overcome it?

On my last day of school, a teacher told me I would never amount to much in life. Yes, it did affect me. It was unexpected and left me confused.

But as Tony Robbins says, "Your worst moments can sometimes turn out to be your greatest gifts." This is true. That moment fired up my rebellious nature, and I started to look for ways to prove the teacher wrong. I had a plan that I would go back to her one day to show her who I'd become, so she'd take back her words. But I don't carry that resentment anymore, since I've learned to credit my teacher for my success. I now have a smile on my face, and there's no charge around that situation. I have appreciation and gratitude. I realise I needed to hear it, as it was the motivation I needed.

What decisions have made a difference in your life?

> It's in your moments of decision that your destiny is shaped"
> *~ Tony Robbins*

There are many decisions that have shaped my life. When I was fifteen my sister, who studied psychology, got me to write down everything I wanted to achieve by the time I turned thirty. At that stage I had no filters or beliefs. I didn't ask why or think it was a difficult exercise to do.

I followed the instruction and wrote out everything I wanted to achieve by the age of thirty. It was probably the best decision I ever made. For each item on my list, I unconsciously moved to achieving what I had written down. I achieved the car, met my beautiful wife, worked at the career of my dreams and moved to Australia, where I'd always wanted to live.

What's the best thing that's ever happened to you and why?

This is so freaky. I'd imagined a move to London and always had an image of Piccadilly Circus with all of the lights. When I moved there, our first stop in London was Piccadilly Circus, and my first image as I exited the tube station was all of the lights flashing brightly. That memory is still in my mind today. What's great is that now I'm completely aware of how and why it happened. It all has to do with the Reticular Activating System (RAS), which is a set of connected nuclei in the brain that's responsible for regulating wakefulness and sleep-wake transitions.

What is your big WHY?

It's simple. I want to share with the world what I've learnt, not because I know it all, but because of how my life has fundamentally shifted over time.

Before I'd done personal development, like I said, I had a lot of conflict. I had the belief I was stupid and that everybody else was cleverer, and I allowed this belief to make me play way below my potential. At times I didn't even bother trying. This also led me to having an inferiority complex. I used to say that when something happened to me it was always somebody else's fault. In my mind, the whole world was against me.

What I ultimately learned was that I was playing out my paradigm, as Bob Proctor refers to it. I realised I was responsible for my results, good or bad. I had a lot of belief systems that weren't serving me. When I changed my beliefs about who I was, my life started expanding, and now I have the awesome privilege to share my journey and impact lives.

Life is simple. It's made complicated by over thinking. A quick tip: don't attempt to mind read or predict the future. Instead, begin to live in the now. All you have control over are the thoughts you have and the actions you take. Everything else is beyond your control.

What do you think is your life purpose? What do you believe you've been put on the planet to do?

I believe I'm living my life purpose. There was a time where if you told me I'd be a Peak Performance Results Coach or a presenter of personal development programs, I would have asked you what planet you were from. However, when I reflect on my journey and what influences I've had in my life, I'm absolutely certain I'm doing what I was meant to do.

When I was probably about fourteen, I inherited my sister's bedroom. It was huge, and I had a proper study desk...not that I studied much. However, I did read a lot. I came across a book by Sigmund Freud that explained psychoanalysis and the placebo effect. I was intrigued by what was written but had no way to put it into context. At that stage of my life, I was ignorant and had no real-life experience.

But it did somehow give me unconscious wisdom that came out while having conversations with friends about relationships and life. Somewhere I'd also had a belief imprinted in my mind that I could achieve anything I wanted to, as I long as I put my mind to it. These philosophies have unconsciously guided me to take actions I wouldn't necessarily have taken if I didn't have this belief system in place.

It's strange that it was only after studying personal development when I realised the impact of these philosophies, and now I know I'm on purpose. Another is that there's no conflict within me about what I'm doing. It feels right, unlike when I was an engineer looking for anything and everything to distract me and take me away from performing my tasks. I'm living my dream.

How are you currently making a difference in people's lives?

I'm living my purpose by being a Peak Performance Results Coach. It's a privilege and an honour to serve Tony's clients, and I've seen some spectacular growth from those who are willing to commit to doing what's required to get results. I coach CEOs, business owners and entrepreneurs. I'm also a licensed LifeSuccess Consultant for Bob Proctor to present and teach a number of his programs and workshops. I've coached in excess of 10,000 sessions.

What are you passionate about?

I'm passionate about inspiring individuals to create a world without boundaries and to encourage them to break through to reveal their true magnificence. This was my mission statement I created in 2004 and am now living. What I learned is to find your passion and then find a way to make an income from it. As the saying goes, do what you love, and you'll never work a day in your life, so that's what I did. I now have reworked my mission statement to be: INSPIRE, IMPACT, TRANSFORM.

What do you think are some of the issues people face in life?

People believe that having problems is the end of the world.

The best explanation I heard was by Tony Robbins at a "Date with Destiny" seminar. He said the only problem people have is that they believe they shouldn't have problems, but problems are gifts, and their purpose is to challenge us and make us grow. He said rather than wishing for no problems, people need to find ways to overcome them.

What's the biggest tip you could give people regarding this issue?

I believe if you accept problems as a part of life, and you learn to deal with them, you will have less stress. I coach a lot of my clients with regards to how they can soften the impact of a so-called problem. For instance, I used to call them challenges. I thought it made me more committed to solving them, but it always felt like hard work. It was only when I remembered a story Tony told about Ken Blanchard calling a problem a situation, that I began to see it differently, and they stopped having a negative charge. So call your problems a situation, and it will give you the ability to deal with them with clarity rather than stress.

What's the biggest mistake people make in goal setting?

You may be surprised when I say this, but I don't believe people set goals they truly want to achieve. My recommendation is to set goals that light you up, so even if they're not easy to achieve, you will find a way.

How can you help people in this area of setting goals?

I help a lot of people in the area of defining their goals. It starts with dreaming and is an easy process.

1. Write down a Dream List of a hundred items of everything you want to BE/DO/HAVE, without limitation and judgement. Don't share it with anybody, unless they're committed to being supportive about you living your true dreams.

2. Take the list and break it down into one and three year goals. Anything beyond three years leave as your dreams.

3. Prioritise the list of one year goals and find your top three.

4. With each of the goals, write down the outcome you desire. This is where you have to apply the acronym S.M.A.R.T.

- **S**pecific

- **M**easurable

- **A**chievable

- **R**ealistic

- **T**ime Frame

A great test of whether you have it right is to ask yourself if you can measure the goal, because if you can't measure the progress or actions you're taking, then the goal isn't specific enough.

5. Ask yourself why it's important for you to achieve this goal. This is your driving force. If you don't have a strong enough why, you will more than likely give up on the goal. This is an important step, however most people don't bother going in depth.

6. Now brainstorm the different ways to achieve the outcome you desire. Remember: the more varied your approach, the more resourceful you will be when facing situations.

7. Chunk your tasks into manageable sizes, so you're able to take action.

8. Take the actions and schedule them into your diary, so you can track your progress.

9. In the future, and as you keep achieving your goals, you will move your dream goals to your three year goals and then to your one year goals.

EXERCISE

1. Take your one year goals, prioritise them and choose your top three goals.

2. Break your one year goals into quarterly goals, which will make them ninety day goals.

3. Take your ninety day goals and break them into 3 x 30 day goals.

4. Take your thirty day goals and break them into 3 x 10 day goals.

5. Determine the actions required, and schedule it into your diary.

6. TAKE ACTION!

How did you become interested in goal setting?

I only became aware of the term goal setting when I started my personal development journey. I had the realisation that I'd been setting goals unintentionally all of my life and wondered how much more powerful it would be if it was a more intentional activity. As Tony

Robbins says, when you begin planning your outcomes in advance, it's not that everything goes to plan, but it has the ability to compress decades into years. That's what's happening in my life, as well as the lives of my clients who do the work and stick to the system.

I set a goal to become a Peak Performance Results Coach at "Unleash the Power Within", and within a year I'd realised that goal. I had no idea how I was going to achieve it. Everyone can set goals. As a matter of fact, you're already doing it, you just don't know it.

How do you go from a concept or idea, to a business?

This is something I work on a lot with my clients. It comes from having a deep desire to have a business, because if you don't, then you might want to reconsider.

You always start from what you're passionate about, because it allows you to position yourself as an expert in that particular area. It also ensures that as you develop the business, you enjoy doing the research and you're familiar with it. This means you can be a little more resourceful when it comes to thinking outside of the box. Also, your knowledge base will be stronger, as you have an interest in the topic.

What's your most inspiring client story?

I have a lot of inspiring stories from clients who've healed miraculously to those who wound up earning ten times their income.

There was one client who was unhappy at work and wanted to leave. We did some coaching to a point where he realized his job was great, and he started to enjoy it, so he was in a good place. If we'd stopped there, my job would have been done.

But we didn't. We started to brainstorm businesses he could start, and all he kept saying was that he didn't have any business ideas. This is when I asked him what he enjoyed doing. He told me, and I suggested we research more about it. The next session we brainstormed some more about his idea, and because he awakened his RAS, he began to find opportunities around it.

To cut a long story short, I coached him to develop an online store and sell his products. Well, he is so successful now and become so busy he's opened up a retail space and left his job. We're now looking at ways to further optimise his business.

All of this came down to the simple question, "What are you most interested in?" Then we looked for ways to turn it into a business.

What's the best way people can achieve a healthy life-work balance?

A good life-work balance breaks up into eight hours for sleep/eight hours for work/eight hours for play. I believe most people can attain this goal if they have a job that pays them for doing eight hours of work per day at a maximum of forty hours a week.

When I was working in a regular job, this was easy to achieve. The only problem is that in order to have true freedom and live a life according to my own set of rules, I knew having a job was not the way to go about it. I'm of the opinion that the only way to achieve true freedom is to set up your own business.

When you work for someone else, you're helping them build their dreams. I'm not saying it's bad, but you need to know the limitations. In most cases, it's important to remember that when you start out in life, you have to be a follower before you become a leader.

So when it comes to a healthy life-work balance, I believe that if you're a new business owner, and have previously worked in a nine-to-five job, it will be a shock to the system. The balance isn't the same when you're a business owner, especially when you're new in business and don't have a structure and support system in place. At first, you'll spend more time working than living. But this is no different from a boss asking you to do overtime and work weekends to get a project completed.

The great thing is that when you're in business for yourself, you can set the rules. However, I find that a lot of business owners fall into the trap of following the same rules as if they were working for someone. When you're a business operator, please realise that you will be doing your normal workload as if you were an employee, as well as the workload of a business owner. In general, you will initially have an unbalanced life-work balance, but as a business owner you can set up and adjust your work, workday and workload to suit your lifestyle. Life-work balance doesn't exist for a business owner, but always keep in mind you're building your own dreams, so what you put in is what you're going to get out.

There are a couple of principles I tend to follow, unless I have major deadlines or commitments.

1. Sleep no less than five hours a day, but know that sleep studies say six to seven hours is best.

2. Plan out your week, month and year ahead, while ensuring you have some down time, For instance, you can use Sundays as a family day.

3. Remember that as a business owner you set the rules, so you can take time out from the business whenever you want. It just takes planning.

4. A healthy life-work balance is whatever you determine works for you, so do what you enjoy and what reenergises you.

5. You're building your dreams, so build your business for the lifestyle you want.

Do you live your love?

Absolutely. There's not one part of what I do that's incongruent. I'm living my dream. Even though I still have other dreams, I will never stop doing what I do. I love my life!

Why is mindset important?

It's the filter by which you experience life. So if you view the world as if it's against you, you're always going to be dissatisfied, disappointed and discontented.

When you control what you think about and the meaning you give to situations, then you can control the way you feel. If you poll most people, you'll find they just want to be happy. But most people place their happiness outside of themselves, which only gives them moments of happiness. You need to recognise it doesn't come from what you do but who you are.

With a creative mindset, you can have the most amazing happiness, even when you're going through the most traumatic times in your life. The right mindset will help you become more resourceful and enable you to find a way, even when it seems impossible to achieve.

How does someone keep inspired on a daily basis?

I coach many a client around this particular area, where they've achieved a certain amount of success in the past, and then they lose the drive. There are a couple of reasons why this happens. One is that they get comfortable with where they are, because they've achieved what they wanted. But what happens is that they don't have any other goals, so they experience something called drift. An easy fix is to understand where they currently are and what their resources are, so they can set a new destination and raise the sails. If you want to be inspired every day, you need to have worthy goals to achieve that will scare and excite you.

Another way is to find a vocation you're passionate about, because then you'll be naturally inspired to take action. I never feel like what I do is a job.

What are some common barriers people have?

Limiting beliefs, paradigms, stories and traditions. The amount of belief you have will directly translate into the outcome you achieve. As Tony Robbins says, "It's the stories you tell yourself that are holding you back from achieving your ultimate outcome."

Understanding how to shift my paradigm has been the key to making huge progress in multiple areas in my life. Without understanding this concept, I would still be stuck in a job being unhappy. It's easier than you think to shift, but you must be prepared to do the work.

What are your tips for getting through a difficult time in life?

1. Start with immediate gratitude that you're still alive and can make decisions.

2. Look for people who've survived and thrived going through a similar, or worse, situation.

3. See the situation for what it truly is, not worse or better, and then find a way to resolve it.

4. Find a reason why it's important to get through difficult times. If you don't have any hope, it will be challenging to keep going.

5. Detach from the outcome, and let go.

Why are goals important?

Without goals

- you're a rudderless vessel in the middle of the ocean, being bashed continuously by your environment
- there's no major inspiration or drive to do what's required to create the life of your dreams
- you will remain in a comfort zone that will bring about immense dissatisfaction and could lead to depression
- you will die earlier

Goals

- give you direction
- move you outside of your comfort zone, where you can be excited about life
- keep you getting out of bed every day
- help you achieve a certain amount of fulfilment in life
- give you a reason and a purpose

What's the best way to set and achieve goals?

It's a simple question that people over-complicate by wondering how they're going to do it, which is the most disempowering question to ask. Here are the steps to take:

1. Start with where you are right now. What resources, skills and knowledge do you have?

2. Decide what you want to achieve.

3. Make it specific and date driven.

4. Find a way to close the gap.

What mindset do you believe is needed to create a great life?

The correct mindset is to know that everything is possible, you just have to find a way. It will allow you to always be resourceful, even when you don't know the next step to take, and be able to find a way to create it.

How do you start your day?

As soon as I wake up, I am thankful for another day where I'm above ground, and I frame everything else as an opportunity and a gift to enjoy.

Does visualisation help in life? Does it work?

Yes. Knowing what you want and reading it out every day will create a movie that will awaken your RAS.

When your RAS is awakened, you will find new opportunities and make decisions that will move you towards living that life. Most people visualise what they don't want, so they don't get what they want.

What do you believe holds most people back from achieving success and the lifestyle they desire?

What they want isn't what they desire, because otherwise they would be making decisions to achieve that lifestyle. Not defining exactly what they want, and not knowing the reason they want it, makes it difficult to take action.

What are your favourite ways to relax and enjoy life?

Strange as it might seem, when I'm doing what I love, mentoring and coaching, I'm enjoying life. I can't think of anything that would give me as much satisfaction and fulfilment as helping people change their lives and take action towards their dreams.

How can people be happier in life?

By not believing that happiness is achieved from outside of themselves. Stop comparing yourself to people who have decades of experience and achievements and be happy with your stage of development.

How can people overcome fear?

By living in the now and making sure they're focussed on what they can control instead of being concerned about what they can't.

F.E.A.R.:

False

Evidence

Appearing

Real

Remember that fear is only a perception, and when you keep it real, you will be able to control your fear.

How do you make the most of your time?

I plan out my entire year by breaking it down into months and weeks, and then days.

The best way to squeeze the most out of your time is to set a series of short ten-day day goals that keep you absolutely focussed.

Give this a go.

1. Take a thirty day goal and break it up into three ten day goals. Then set your daily actions.
2. At the beginning of each day, record what you plan to do, and at the end of the day, record what you've done.

You'll be surprised how much you're able to achieve. I had a client use this formula to complete in three days what he thought it would take ten to do.

What's the best way for someone to transform their life?

This is the advice I was given when I first started on my journey:

Go to your nearest library, become a member and get literature that will inspire you to:

- READ
- LISTEN
- APPLY

What was the one thing that when you got it, everything else seemed to fall into place?

After I realised my paradigms had been programmed into me since birth and included some empowering and disempowering beliefs, it led to knowing I was responsible for the way I felt and that nobody could make me feel anything I didn't want to.

Ivor Lok

What does success mean to you?

I believe it's best summed up by this quote from Tony Robbins:

> "Success is doing what you want, when you want, where you want, with whom you want, as much as you want."

 To discover more about how Ivor can help you *Elevate Your Success*, visit

www.elevate-books.com/success

Samith Pich
Online Success

Samith is a successful internet marketer, online business and marketing coach, speaker and trainer. He helps heart-centred businesses conquer the internet, so they can grow and prosper in the digital age.

Samith has been fortunate to have worked with large, multinational businesses and solo entrepreneurs, helping them to grow their businesses and brands online. His digital agencies have run over a million dollars in digital marketing campaigns for clients in Australia, the United States and across the ASEAN region.

Samith lives in Perth, Western Australia, with his much-loved wife and three daughters.

Samith Pich

Online Success

What drives you?

Gratitude and service are what drive me. It's a journey that started thousands of miles away from where I am today.

More than thirty years ago, my family and I fled a terrible civil war in my birth country of Cambodia. We arrived on the shores of Western Australia as refugees facing an uncertain future. Scarred by loss and personal tragedy like so many before them, my parents came with nothing but the shirts on their backs. The heaviest items they carried were their dreams of a better life for all of us.

Compared to others, my family and I were poor, but I never felt we lacked for anything. Though my mother and father worked hard and scrimped and saved, there was always a feeling of immense, quiet gratitude. Our home might have been a fragile, beaten-down rental, yet we believed it was a castle. And it was.

With such good fortune to be alive and have the opportunities of living in a safe, prosperous country with jobs and education, our parents' focus became tempered with how we could make the most of this opportunity. How could one who has been given so much, give back? This became our mission, a service of love. It's a practice we continue to this day.

What's been your biggest life lesson?

"Just be yourself, because everyone else is already taken." These inspirational and genuinely funny words by Oscar Wilde sum up for me the secret to personal success.

Online Success

In a sea of conformity and a society of *Me, too!* sometimes it's difficult to just be yourself. Growing up with my Cambodian heritage, brown skin, big teeth and gravity-defying hair, I longed for nothing more than to fit in.

On the outside I was a happy-go-lucky kid, but on the inside I often felt ashamed of myself. I was embarrassed by my quiet nature and introversion. By my love of history, art and books and not being *sporty* or *manly* enough. I spent the good part of my young adult years second guessing every natural inclination.

It wasn't until the age of twenty-eight when I read Oscar's wise words, and their truth finally struck a chord in me to rediscover myself.

Just being yourself relies on a hard-won quality not enough people possess. That's the quality of self-acceptance. Before you can just be you and grow in confidence, you need to accept yourself, warts and all. But acceptance only comes when you're really clear on what's important to you. When you feel it in your bones. I've learned so many lessons, but the one regarding self-acceptance, of just being okay to be me, has been the most empowering, profitable and gratifying.

If you were speaking to your younger self, what advice would you give?

Your soft qualities will be your most potent. You are stronger beyond measure when you have love in your heart. Your love will move mountains when you realise what's most important to you.

Just be yourself, because that's when you're at your most powerful, congruent and affecting, and you will be loved in return.

You're a big-picture guy, and that's a great quality to have, but take a few moments before you rush headlong into your next project to consider the small details. Not honouring them could break you.

Opportunities are like buses. There's always another coming along. Use your head, but follow your heart when making decisions. If you always come from a place of love, it won't ever lead you astray.

And for heaven's sake, clean up your room!

What were your views around money when growing up, and how did they change?

My parents loved us, but they knew nothing about money. After coming from a poverty-stricken, war-torn country, I don't blame them. My father was a gambler, and my mother was a hoarder. It kind of explains why I spent many years taking risks and cluttering up my life.

For them, money was hard to come by. They worked hard and sacrificed it on the one thing they felt mattered most of all: education. Getting a good education was the gateway to a better life and the key to prosperity. It was important to receive good grades and go to an exceptional university in order to get a high-paying job.

It seemed like a recipe for success, and I followed it, until one day I woke up depressed and bankrupt, with someone in uniform repossessing my car and the food I ate consisting of what I begged for from the Salvation Army. That night as I had my dinner, I cried at the table.

It wasn't until later that I came to realise I knew absolutely nothing about money.

While the key to success started with education, it wasn't enough. I became fascinated by success and wealth, mainly out of desperation to get out of my present situation. I learned the innate, immutable laws of money and prosperity, which is that it all started with mindset and a personal philosophy.

Another key distinction I uncovered was that no one gets truly wealthy from working a nine-to-five. Essentially, ninety-seven percent of truly wealthy people all had their own businesses. In order to be successful, I needed to be a business owner. After much research, I decided on an online business.

What's the worst thing that's ever happened to you, and how did you overcome it?

Becoming bankrupt, emotionally and financially, when I was twenty-eight. My first marriage also ended during the same time, and I went from a high school arts teacher's wage to becoming a single father of two girls and living on welfare.

It wasn't just the horrible and messy separation or the utter bankruptcy and its subsequent humiliation of moving back with my parents, it was that I'd truly lost myself. I felt like a ghost in my own life.

What got me to overcome it all was the unconditional love of my family. Over time, their love would bring me back to life. One day I started writing and printing out affirmations and positive sayings and placing them in pertinent places in our house.

My favourite quote was by Albert Camus:

"In the midst of winter, I found there was, within me, an invincible summer."

And I did find that invincible summer within me, as well.

What's the best thing that's ever happened to you and why?

The birth of my three daughters and marrying my wife, Iris. They teach me about love and acceptance and challenge me to be the best father, husband and man they deserve. I wake up every day filled with gratitude that I get to share this one precious life together with them.

What were some aha moments that changed everything for you?

Some of my favourite aha moments came from listening to bootlegged copies of Jim Rohn's early audio seminars in my beat-up Hyundai Excel as I drove to relief teaching gigs. Here are some of my favourite quotes:

- *"Success is something you attract by becoming an attractive person."*

- *"It's not the blowing of the wind that determines your destination, it's the set of the sail."*

- *"Unless you change, nothing changes."*

- *"Work harder on yourself than you do your job."*

To sum it up in a sentence, these seminars opened my mind to a new world of being and living. Sometimes I would stop my car by a park just to replay those words and imagine Jim Rohn sitting in the passenger seat beside me giving advice in his homespun, folksy manner. All of a sudden the hardships I was facing no longer mattered so much. My present conditions were inconsequential. All that mattered was where I was going and where I was setting my sail. At a time when I had so little, it stoked the fire inside of me to imagine and do more.

What decisions have made a difference in your life?

There's a great scene in the Disney movie, *The Incredibles*, where Edna Mole talks about her philosophy on life and fashion. "I never look back, darling. It distracts from the now."

So, the biggest decisions I've made in my life centred around forgiveness and letting go. That means letting go of past hurts, imagined or real. When I finally let go and forgave others, and most importantly myself, it gave me the mental room to put a hundred percent of my focus on the now.

Who inspires you, and how do they fuel your passion?

The people who most inspire me are those who feel a calling to do and give more. Those who run heart-centred businesses that are keen to upset the status quo and envisage a more humane and prosperous society. I feel it's my mission to help this tribe of people create an online business that not only provides a living but can also create a life for them and their families.

When someone is empowered financially, they're able to more fully express and live their love. They become servant leaders rather than struggling takers. The world needs more leaders. Empowering others to be their own leaders is my passion.

Why should people learn about elevating themselves online?

We live in an incredible moment in history. It's a time of unprecedented and accelerating change, when problems seem to outweigh solutions. But it's also a time of immense opportunity for the few who are willing to tackle the challenges head on.

Never before in human history have ordinary people been given access to tools and resources that a few decades ago were only available at prohibitive prices to large, multinational corporations and a select few. The internet has become the greatest income leveller the world has ever known. What this means is that if you have an idea or a service that helps people or makes them happy, or if you have a talent, a calling or even a hobby, then you can easily start an online business that can access a potential worldwide audience.

It doesn't matter if you're an aspiring filmmaker, writer, songstress, quilt maker or dog trainer. The world wants what you have.

How did you become interested in internet marketing and helping elevate others online?

There are two factors that move people into action: inspiration and desperation. I fall into the second category.

When I came back home after my separation and bankruptcy, I settled back into contract teaching in order to make a living. But as the bills grew, I came to realise that doing what I'd always done would only lead to getting what I had always got. I realised I needed a way out of the nine-to-five. I no longer wanted my income to be chained to my time, and I didn't want to be told what to do, when to do it and who to say please to. So it wasn't long before I found internet marketing and making money online. I started to dream again that I could finally provide a good life for my family and be able to spend more time with them.

It looked simple enough. I saw lots of pictures of fast cars, laptop lifestyles, big cheques and push-button riches. Reality, however, was nothing like the commercials. For the next four years I struggled online. I spent thousands of dollars on different programs and buying course after course, as well as lots of push-button software. I suffered long periods of shiny *object-itis*, information overload and procrastination. To overcome my feelings of being overwhelmed, I spent money like a drunken sailor, which dug my family into further credit card debt.

If there was some harebrained scheme on the internet guaranteed to lose me money, I made sure I had my name on it.

When did the situation start to change for you in your online journey?

▸ At some point I had to stop and take a breather. By 2012 I got my first coach who simply asked me, "What's your Why, Samith?"

- I said, "Well, to make money, of course!"

- Then he gently asked again what the real reason was, and I dug in deep as I talked about my Why, and tears came down my face.

I realized my WHY was that I wanted to give my wife the choice to not work and be a fulltime mum. I wanted to stop missing out on my daughters' childhood and be able to pick up from school and take a day off to just be with them. My WHY was to help support my mum in her retirement and look after my family in Cambodia. My WHY is to give back by setting up schools for numeracy and literacy in disadvantaged areas.

That's my WHY.

- *I learnt to pay the price.*

- I didn't always pay it every day, or even perfectly, but I learnt to start paying it effectively. In my previous four years online I'd made around fifty dollars in total. By the end of 2012 I had my first thousand--dollar month, then my first thousand-dollar week, and then my first five, ten and twenty-thousand dollar months.

- In 2013 I quit teaching, and I never looked back.

What is internet marketing?

Internet marketing, or online marketing, refers to advertising and marketing efforts that use the web and email to drive direct sales. However, there's no singular approach to internet marketing, mainly due to the vast number of platforms, strategies and methods that encompass several disciplines.

Overall, I prefer Copyblogger's definition of online marketing as, "Building authority using content to inform and build trust with prospects and customers." In the information age, content is king. And if you can master the art of delivering high value and good content, you're more likely to increase authority, build trust and make sales.

How does someone start an online business?

The fundamentals of starting an online business are really no different from a brick-and-mortar business. You need the following:

1. A product that solves a problem, caters to a need or gives people what they want.

2. A group of people who are hungry to solve that problem, fulfil that need or get that product/ service.

3. A way to process, get or deliver that service or product to the customer.

When you have these essentials, you can then go about building your online empire.

These are the six essential elements to any online businesses.

1. Get a domain name.

   ▸ I use services like Namecheap. Think of it as the online address of your future storefront. At a minimum, I encourage everyone to register their own name as a domain, such as www.samithpich.com. This helps brand you. The other choice is a brand name, which would be the name of the company you establish.

2. Obtain domain hosting.

   ▸ A couple of suggestions are Bluehost or Justhost. Think of this as your virtual plot of land where your future online shop, service or training will be housed.

3. Make a website.

- This is your actual shopfront, where you will house your content and offerings. You will need to decide what the structure of your business will be. For instance, whether it's an ecommerce shopping site, a blog, an information site or a branding site. One platform that's versatile, yet strong, is the WordPress platform. It's customisable and easy to use. All you have to do is choose a theme that dictates how your site will look.

4. Get an email service provider (ESP).

- A couple of examples would be Getrseponse.com or Aweber.com. This provides a way to collect emails and contact details via an opt-in form or squeeze page, as well as follow up with your potential customers. What's nifty about this is you can schedule your follow-up emails ahead of time, so they go out automatically.

5. Get involved in social media platforms.

- Social media has revolutionised the way people interact and share meaningful content. The biggest platform continues to be Facebook, but there's also Twitter, LinkedIn, Instagram and Pinterest. For your own sanity, don't feel compelled to join every platform in the beginning.

6. Get a payment processor like Paypal or Stripe.

- These services allow you to process credit card payments online.

  There are a thousand different plug-ins, online tools, widgets and apps you can add to your website or business to make it more functional, but it all depends on your business. Online marketing is a lot like applying makeup. In the beginning, less is more.

Are there any real systems or ways to get rich quick online?

Yes there are, and here it is: solve more problems.

The most fulfilling action anyone can take is to connect deeply with another person and solve some type of problem they're having. Therefore, if you want to be rich and fulfilled, make it your duty to serve others by solving as many of their problems related to your purpose as possible.

My mentor taught me that you get paid in proportion to the number of people you affect. If you want to get rich, simply affect more people. The internet is a wonderful tool to help you do that. When you put something online that inspires, empowers, educates or simply entertains the masses, it can quickly go viral. The internet allows you affect people exponentially and to *get rich quick* in three to five years, compared to the traditional way of working forty hours a week for forty years to live on a retirement that may or may not be there when the time comes. This is the quickest and most ethical way to get rich quick there is!

Do you need to be a techie to start an online business?

This may surprise you, but the answer is no. I'm definitely not a techie, and when I first started I barely used email. The good news is that if you decide to learn, the tools are easier and more user friendly than ever, and there are tons of free tutorials for every widget doo-hickey out there. Yes, that's the technical term.

I would invest a small amount of time to just get an overview of the essentials and basics. This helps you have a competent idea of the process if you ever decide to outsource the job. However, I would caution any aspiring entrepreneur in using up all of their time learning every technical facet of their business. Unless your core business is about knowing how to create and program large e-commerce sites from scratch, then get a professional to do it.

Keep your focus on the core revenue-generating activities.

What's the most important resource to finding success online?

Your mindset and your own personal philosophies are your most important resources. They're either empowering and elevating you or they're hindering and holding you back. But specifically you need an entrepreneurial/ business mindset rather than an employee mindset. It's easy to change your mindset, because it's usually the one you've grown up with. But with the right education, understanding your Why and coaching, it can be shifted.

What are the most common traps people fall into when it comes to internet marketing?

Most people are great learners but not great implementers. The main reason is that when you implement something, there's a high probability of failure. You're taught from a young age that failure is bad, but to entrepreneurs it's crucial. Failure is the crucible against which entrepreneurs cut their teeth. It provides one of the most coveted qualities in business: experience.

Many would-be entrepreneurs are too scared of failure, so they keep on learning and never implementing. This leads to information overload and shiny object syndrome. As a recovering procrastinator myself, I know all too well the trap that is *perfection-itis*.

How do you go from a concept or idea to a business?

You don't have to be the next Apple or Coca-Cola to be successful online. Start off with an intention such as, *Seek the underserved market and serve them*. It starts by being open and sensitive to the problems of others.

There's an old adage in business: the customer has the answers. To get the ball rolling, use simple online surveys that will help you find problems and seek validation about your ideas. Once you find a market gap and an expression of interest, get to work as quickly as possible on a minimally viable product (MVP). This could be a quick online course, a taster of the final product or a small service.

Some of my most successful courses were first sold before they were ready. I tested whether the idea was what the market wanted by seeing how many people bought the idea. Then I fulfilled the order.

My biggest tip is to move fast and make mistakes faster. Money loves speed. Success loves action. Don't wait until all of your ducks line up. One, they probably never will be, and two, by the time they do, the opportunity has disappeared.

What are the most important components of any online business?

These are the five core components of any online business. This is a brief overview. More can be found in my trainings and coaching and on my website.

1. Content Strategy

    - There's a saying online that *content is king*. Well it's also queen and everything in between. Becoming a content creator is a marketing strategy that helps attract your target audience, as well as build your authority, trust and likeability factor. It's because people want to do business with people they like, know and trust. The most common way to create content is via blogs, videos, social media, podcasts, books, and speaking.

    - One tip I'd like to give is to be intentional about the content you provide. As far as a marketing strategy, your goal should be to attract, acquire and engage your audience. Your content needs to be purposeful and strategic.

2. Lead generation

Your email list is still your most valuable business asset online, only surpassed by a customer/ buyers list. To begin lead generation you only need the following:

- A lead magnet, also known as an ethical bribe. It entices the prospect to give their email details in exchange for a free e-book, course or video.

- An opt-in form. This is where the prospect puts their email address.

- An email auto-responder service. It collects the email address and provides a platform to follow up later.

3. Follow up

- Follow up is important, since nine out of ten, people won't buy the first time they ask about your product or service, and it takes on average seven or eight exposures to create a customer. Repeat after me: *the fortune is in the follow up*.

- When you follow up in an engaging, entertaining and educational manner that leads to conversions, it helps build rapport, trust and authority.

4. Monetisation strategy

- Aka, *How are you going to make money?* You need to offer the customer more reasons to buy, because you solve more problems for them. As long as you keep solving problems, they will be happy to buy from you.

- A decent monetisation strategy should have multiple tiers or price points: low, mid and high. Ideally, you should try to include a reoccurring service to attract a passive income.

5. Traffic

- Traffic is another term for visitors to your website. My big tip is to master one traffic source first.

- There are essentially three types of traffic sources:

- Free, such as search engine optimisation, blogging, video and social media

- Paid, such as Google Adwords, Facebook ads, pay per click and banner ads

- The traffic you own, such as your email list, YouTube subscribers and your Facebook groups

What were your biggest mistakes in starting an online business?

The biggest mistake I've personally made is not building a list earlier. List building means generating a following of email subscribers. There are many affiliate marketing methods where you don't have to build a list, but then you're always at the mercy of a changing platform or traffic source. I would have made so much more money if I'd started building a list earlier and followed them up with value and offers.

The other big mistake is doing or starting too much at once. *Focus* is the biggest key to success in the beginning. Master one traffic source. Focus your energy on one business model and one income stream until you're successful in that area. Then move on.

My last big mistake was not hiring a coach or mentor early on, because I was stingy. I made many business mistakes and lost time and money trying multiple strategies. Most wound up not working. I know I would have cut my time in half and doubled my results if I'd gotten a coach in the beginning.

How can someone find their life purpose?

Paradoxically, the best way for someone to find their life purpose is to stop looking for it. To find yourself you need to give yourself permission to stop and be silent. Your purpose is always talking to you, so you just need to make time to find a quiet place and listen to your heart.

You might find it helpful to start a meditation practice or take up yoga. Personally, I like to go and sit by the beach around sunset and watch the waves and sky. I've also found clarity when I consciously block out external noise while I'm driving or having a run. It's a simple practice that makes room for an inner dialogue with your true self. Sometimes I ask it a question to prod the process. Most of the time, it prods me.

When you go into the world and do everything with enthusiasm and full commitment, you will undoubtedly experience moments of clarity, love, fulfilment, and gratitude. You will be your best you, and that will be enough.

Do what you love, and put love into what you do. Immerse yourself in learning everything you can about what you're most inspired by, and then go out there and provide value in the world. When you love what you do, you will be living your purpose.

How does someone keep inspired on a daily basis?

I don't think everyday inspiration is necessary. It can become an addiction. For instance, watching motivational videos instead of taking action. It detracts from the actual *doing of the thing*. Success is ninety-nine percent perspiration and one percent inspiration, in that ratio. If you need someone to keep you inspired and motivated all of the time, then you're probably not doing what you love.

Having said that, I will admit I'm often inspired by the results of my, and my students', work, and that encourages me to do more of it. I work from a place of a deep-centred Why. It's like a heartbeat or a profound current in the ocean. It's barely noticeable, but it moves everything.

What are your tips for getting through a difficult time in life?

Know that it passes, and it helps to have someone you can get support from, even if it's only a kind ear.

To think that tough times last forever is to misunderstand nature and the seasons of life. Tough times don't last, but tough people do, and you'll be stronger for having gone through it. Usually time does heal all wounds and circumstances change naturally, but most of the time it takes a conscious effort to learn from the root cause of your mistakes and take the necessary action to get yourself out of it.

Also, realise that life is kinda perfect. Often the hardest times set you up for the best of times. They become springboards from which major learning arrives. They cultivate wisdom.

Realise that within every hardship and pain, there's a seed of opportunity and blessing. You must dig and search for it.

What mindsets do you believe are needed to create a great business/life?

- A humble mindset that sees the abundance in everything.
- A giving mindset that's open to receiving.
- A master's mindset that loves to learn.
- *I learnt that this business is a business of self-determination.*
- But it's not about faking it till you make it. It's about stepping into your greatness, always working on yourself and seeking to give more value than you receive in return.

What are some tools or strategies you could recommend for keeping balance in life?

- Keep a journal that's predominantly about expressing gratitude.

- Treat your body like it's your best friend.

- Treasure people over things, not vice versa.

- Read great books to give you insight and perspective.

- If you lead with light and love, only good can come out of it.

- Laugh lots, especially at yourself.

What was the one thing that when you got it, everything else seemed to fall into place?

I *got* that I was worthy and had a story worthy of sharing. Also that by sharing what made me special, I helped and inspired others to see their worth as well.

The quality of life comes down to the quality of the stories you tell about it. From experience, you create both the stories and the meaning behind them. Tell a disempowered, victim story, and that's what you become. Tell a story about overcoming odds and being an inspiration, and that's what you are. Your life is the story you write, so go write a good one!

Any last words of advice for those looking to start an online business?

- Don't get into an online business for the money. Have a greater Why.

- Business is simple: create value for others and then provide a way for people to show their appreciation via paying you for your products and services.

- If you don't feel you have value, either look harder and invest more in yourself to become more valuable, or learn to better communicate your value.

- Internet marketing isn't the business silver bullet. Providing value is.

- You will only get so far thinking about yourself and your wants. When you put your focus on genuinely helping and serving others, you'll go much further financially, emotionally and spiritually.

If you ever need any help in your online journey, feel free to reach out to me at the link below.

To your success.

 To discover more about how Samith can help you *Elevate Your Success*, visit www.elevate-books.com/success

Fiona Jones
PassionPreneur

Fiona Jones is a nine-times bestselling author, publisher, authorpreneur and speaker. She began her professional life as a medical sonographer and radiographer but later turned her passion from the medical to the business world and created *Author Express*, a program developed to educate those interested in sharing their knowledge and message through a professionally published book.

Her mission is to inspire millions. *Be Your Own Success Story* is her motto, and she believes this is done by doing what you're passionate about, sharing your message, making a difference and leaving a legacy.

Fiona lives on thirteen gorgeous acres with her husband, two children and countless animals.

Fiona Jones

PassionPreneur

What does PassionPreneur mean, and what is a PassionPreneur?

It's a combination of the words passion and entrepreneur. PassionPreneurs are people who make a living doing what they're passionate about.

I've loved every job, career or business I've had, and for a long time I didn't realise people went to work in jobs they didn't like, just to pay the bills. The funny thing is these same people then say money isn't important, yet they exchange hours for money five days a week doing something they don't enjoy.

I would love to see more people starting their journey to become a PassionPreneur.

How can someone get started doing what they love?

One of my favourite quotes is, "You don't have to see the whole staircase, you just have to take the first step."

This could never be truer than starting your own business. None of my endeavours have started with a mission statement, a business plan, an MBA in business, or even a simple business course.

The universe rewards action. When you take the first step in faith, the next step will be shown. You will be given signs or signposts. Here are some examples:

- You find the person you need for the next step, such as a real estate agent, architect, builder, graphic designer, mentor or web designer.

- The business or product name will pop into your head.
- The product or materials you need will be on sale.
- You overhear a conversation where someone mentions a great shop for lease or an invitation will show up in your email inbox.
- An advertisement in a newspaper will appear to leap out at you.

If you don't take the first step, the next one won't reveal itself. Sitting and meditating all day and waiting for an idea to land in your lap won't manifest the business for you. However, if you meditate or visualise before taking action on each part of the journey, it will. Not every step will be smooth, and not every sign will be the right one. That's part of the game. It will be tempting to seize the first offer or person that comes across your path, even though it doesn't *feel* quite right. Trust your instincts.

Jack Canfield meditated to come up with *Chicken Soup for the Soul®*. Everyone he spoke to tried to convince him to change the title. They told him short stories wouldn't sell, but he trusted himself, and after 144 rejections he finally found someone to publish his book. The series went on to become the publishing phenomenon of the decade.

Steve Jobs said it best in his Stanford commencement speech. If you haven't seen it, I recommend you watch it on YouTube. This part is powerful:

"Your time is limited, so don't waste it living someone else's life. Don't be trapped by dogma — which is living with the results of other people's thinking. Don't let the noise of others' opinions drown out your own inner voice. And most important, have the courage to follow your heart and intuition. They somehow already know what you truly want to become. Everything else is secondary."

So many people told me not to start my own business. The common phrases I heard were: "You have no business experience," and "You don't have any staff" and "You don't know anything about it". Last but not least, they'd say, "Most businesses fail." My male accountant at the time just gave me one of those looks like, *Yeah right, as if this is going to work.* Running up against this kind of negativity made me more determined to succeed, and I really felt it was all going to be okay. I felt inspired to create a business, and nothing anybody said could stop me.

Forget the competition. Run your own race in your own laneway. Looking at what others do is wasting your time and energy, takes you away from being you and prevents you from getting started. Do what you're passionate about, not what your parents want you to be. Not what you chose and perhaps got a degree in twenty years ago. You're allowed to try something else. Listen to your own inner voice and trust your instincts, because when you do, you will be living life on purpose. That, to me, is success.

Just take the first step.

How do you go from a concept or idea to a successful business?

Recently I was on vacation in Hawaii. Now, I'm not sure if it was getting hit smack in the chest by a falling coconut, which by the way was unbelievably painful and took my breath away, but after this incident I realised for the first time that I'd actually created three businesses to date, and each of them had generated six figures in the first twelve to eighteen months.

Firstly I want to say I had zero experience before starting each of these businesses. In fact, my university degree was in medical imaging, and I spent the majority of my career doing obstetric sonography on pregnant women, which I loved with all my heart.

I'd read the book *Rich Dad, Poor Dad*, and although I was highly paid in my career, I knew I was swapping time for money, and I learnt that if I wanted to achieve real wealth I would need to have a business and other investments. So along with investing in property and creating wealth through renovating small boutique developments, I decided to start a business.

There's no better feeling than taking a little bit of inspiration, a simple idea, and turning it into a real-life creation, whether it's a book, a building, or a business. Creating and inspiring others is my passion.

▸ Business #1

I was living on the sunny Gold Coast where everyone wears bikinis, when the idea of owning a specialist Brazilian waxing salon came to me. I decided to set up and create a brand and a business. After heaps of brainstorming, the name and logo, *Bella Brazilian*®, was born.

I then set out to find a shop and some beauty therapists, even though I had not one single client at the time. I'd read lots of books, though, and found out that most people tend to buy themselves a job rather than building or creating a business. I knew I needed to work on my business and not in it.

I found a great location with lots of trendy cafes and restaurants, a hair salon and a vacant, modern shop that had previously been home to three failed businesses. I used the negotiation skills I learnt from property investing to negotiate a great commercial lease, even though I'd never done this before and didn't fully understand the option terms, which I later found out added a lot of value to the business.

The owner of the shop was interstate and didn't know about the local road works that were severely affecting the area, forcing several businesses to close. In my (basic) business plan, I explained about this and other factors that led to my offer on the rent, rather than just presenting a figure plucked from the sky. I was both excited and a little bit fearful when the owner agreed, and we signed the lease. As a new business owner with no experience, I would not be able to get a business loan, so I redrew on one of my mortgages to fund the fit-out.

The shop was great. It was in an excellent location and space, so we decided to make it into a six room salon. An architect friend designed the interior for me, and my husband and a builder got together and did the fit-out at a fraction of the cost of a shop-fitting company. This allowed us to buy the best salon software package available at the time with a great database system, which enabled us to text clients, a practice that's now commonplace.

I also negotiated every item we had to purchase for the salon and *tried* not to get emotional over whether the disposable underpants were pink or white (pink is my favourite colour, but the pink ones were ten times the price, so forget it.) I knew that every cent I expended would affect the bottom line. After employing our first beautician, we wanted to keep her, and she needed money, so I employed her until we opened. She did anything from painting and cleaning to shopping for knick-knacks.

At the start I paid her from my own wage as an ultrasonographer until we actually opened. At that time I was reading *The E-myth* and *Think and Grow Rich* by Napoleon Hill, and what I learned is that I needed to imagine myself providing the product or service, getting a return for it, and state what I wanted the turnover to be in dollar amounts.

I did just that. I imagined happy customers feeling great and all of the fifty dollar notes going into the cash till. You can imagine my surprise when the turnover for the first year was exactly what I'd written down, even though I'd never thought of it again.

The salon took off from day one, thanks to good old-fashioned service that outclassed our competitors and some unique marketing strategies. One of the best ideas we had was to give our clients a bottle of water after their treatment. The water bottles had our hot pink logo and contact details. People would refill them and use them over and over, and we used to get new clients phoning and saying they got our number off a friend's water bottle. The clients also loved receiving the complimentary water after their visit, as most stores were charging about three dollars at the time.

I loved my time in that business. The experiences I had and the people I met have led me to the path I'm on now. The financial reward after selling the business, that resulted from an offer too good to refuse, allowed me to spend the following three years doing whatever I liked. Had I not listened to my own inner voice and let myself be swayed by the opinions of others, I would have missed out on this experience.

The salon has recently celebrated its tenth birthday, and I feel proud every time I drive by to see its longevity and the continued success of the new owner.

▸ **Business #2**

I had an injury due to the nature of my work as a medical ultrasonographer, which meant I had to leave the career I loved. I went in search of something I could do to replace that income, and I attended a bunch of free seminars. At one of them, the speaker said that everyone has a book inside of them. I had no desire to write one, but the idea that you could create a business from a book, or add a book into a business, excited me.

Without knowing what I was even going to write about, I made a decision to invest $25k in my education and become a published author.

What I found through attending those free seminars was that I was in love with the story behind how the speaker started with nothing and created wealth.

The seed was planted to create The Millionaire book® series and later the Millionaire School®.

Once again, I was in a situation where I had zero contacts and didn't know anyone to interview. I just started searching on Google and in business magazines. I had to get over a lot of fear when I started the book series, as I had to contact people who were on the *BRW* rich list and ask them to be featured in my book. I had to get over rejections and go outside of my comfort zone more times than I can remember. It was the best personal development program I could have received, that's for sure. This is what I love about business. It's real-life personal development, because you suddenly have to acquire skills and ask for money and generally create something from nothing.

I had a system where I could sell copies of the books before I even printed them, so I was able to fund the entire project. I had an outcome and a strategy from the start. The series would be about the business behind the books and not simply selling books.

I published nine books in that series and have inspired a lot of people along the way by sharing success stories. As an extension of the series, I formed the *Millionaire School*, which is a platform for me to share my mentors with others. I loved my *Millionaire* journey and have met so many amazing people who've become lifelong friends.

The initial idea to franchise that business didn't progress as planned, and as time went on I came to realise it wasn't a business model that excited me. In fact, my goal was to use this valuable information and fold it into my next business, which was a lot more exciting to me.

▶ **Business #3**

My third, and current, business, *Author Express*®, came about from constantly being approached by people who wanted to write and publish their own book. After helping over a hundred people become published authors through the *Millionaire* book series, I was meeting a demand of a hungry audience of people wanting to become authors. This was about taking the story that's inside of everyone and showing them the exact steps to get it into the world in the form of a published book. This is something I absolutely love doing.

I developed an education program called *Author Express: From Inspiration to Publication in 5 simple steps.* Below is an infographic of the simple five step system.

For more details on each of the five steps, go to *www.authorexpress.com* and download your free copy of the *Author Express Blueprint: The Ultimate Guide Create, Publish and Promote Your Book.*

The name, *Author Express* ®, came about after heaps of brainstorming on the desired outcome. One was for people to become published authors, which is the **Author** part of the name. The **Express** part actually has a dual meaning. One has to do with the fastest way to publish a professional book (meaning not just an eBook), and the other was for the author to *express* themselves and share their unique message, story or expertise.

We have a range of products and services under the Author Express brand to suit the needs of our clients and result in a professionally published book. I see a lot of books that aren't professionally published and haven't been designed in a way that will grow a brand or a business, which can do the same kind of damage that sending out poor quality video or audio can. While being a perfectionist isn't a requirement for attracting quality clients, it's important to produce quality products.

When a book is published in a way that best represents who you are and what you offer, it can position you for amazing media exposure and act as a leveraged asset in your business, much like you'd receive from a professionally designed website consisting of educational material. You can then follow that up and use your book as a launching pad for seminars, workshops, retreats, consulting and speaking gigs. The list is endless!

Once the book is complete, I then encourage my authors to learn the art of repurposing the information by producing an eBook, audiobook and perhaps even a podcast to extend their audience reach.

That's why I love this process so much. What you're putting out is so much more than a book. It's the transformation you experience in the process of becoming an author, much like the journey of becoming a millionaire. But it's not about the money, it's who you become in the process. So many people get incredible clarity, whether they have an existing business or use the book to start up a business, as they go through the Author Express system. They come to understand it's all about that big vision and making sure the book is positioned for the business behind it. In other words, it acts like a *business card*.

As I like to say, it's not about *selling* a book, it's about *having* a book. Being a published author affects your position and credibility. In effect it means customers and clients seek you out. You've become the go-to person in your niche, since you're the author of the book, and people love to work with *the person who wrote the book*. These days, having a book is the new black.

If you want to learn more about how you can become a published author and cross it off your bucket list, feel free to grab my free author starter pack at *www.authorexpress.com*.

I would love to help you join the dots and show you the exact steps to get that book out of you and into the world.

▶ **Business #4**

While I have no immediate plans to create another business at this stage, since I get my creative fix by helping others publish their book, I know for sure that whatever I do in the future will be a combination of my passion and serving others. To me, having a business and creating a brand is about a niche group of people who want to hang out with you and learn what you know, and then are inspired to help others do the same. The more people who can start doing what they love and showing others it's possible, the better the difference you make in the world. Fulfilment comes when you ask the question, "How can I serve?" not "How can I make money?" I believe everyone is ultimately looking for a life of fulfilment and meaning.

Getting back to getting hit with that coconut, I can say that along with realising how many successful business I've had, my epiphany was also about how I'm doing what I love and that all of my businesses have been about living my passion rather than focussing on making money.

Why do so many people who want to write a book never take action?

To begin with, they simply don't know the first step to take. Whenever you start something new and unknown, part of your brain is designed to protect you and keep you in your comfort zone by sending warning signs like *DANGER! It's the UNKNOWN!* In life, everything you want is on the other side of your comfort zone. Stay there if you want, but know that nothing amazing will come to you by staying safe. Is it uncomfortable going through it? Of course it is. The sad fact is that most people don't take the first step, so they never achieve their dreams.

Firsts are always the hardest: first baby, first house you build, first business you start and first book you write. A lot of the authors I work with go on to create multiple books, because it's much easier once you know how and follow a system.

I think it also comes down to self-love and self-worth. Resistance pops up, and the little voices in your head start saying, *Who will want to read your book? You have nothing new to say* or *I don't like writing* or *I'm not a writer*. Well, I'm not a writer, either. I just follow a system to organise and order my knowledge, which is all a book is. People get so caught up in the details and don't take the first step. Find a mentor who's done what you want to achieve, so they can help guide you through the steps. This will save you time and costly mistakes. Also, many people let their book die inside of them, because they're waiting for it to be perfect. It never will be, so let that go right at the start. I've seen many bestselling, hugely successful books with spelling mistakes or some kind of error.

Just start your book, and your beliefs can catch up later. The universe conspires to help those who take action. I've learnt that the only way to overcome resistance is to sit down and just do that which will lead you to fulfilling your dream.

To write your book, type one word, and then another. Before you know it, you'll have a sentence, then a paragraph, then a page and at last, a chapter. Merely starting the process will overcome resistance and get you in the flow.

You'll probably wonder why you procrastinated at all. You might actually enjoy seeing your word count increase at the end of your session. And if you don't like typing, or it's a slow process for you, with the myriad of technology available you can literally type with your voice.

Give yourself permission to create your book. By organising and ordering your information, you will become an author.

Some people have a fear of success and think they may be too busy and stretched too thin. I know for me as a busy mum and business owner, the fear of success (not wanting to be overwhelmed) has held back the growth of my business in the past. What I know now is that you're only given what you ask for and are capable of. You can create a team of people who love what they do, while you do what you love and value, and together you can make your dream a reality.

When you help enough people get what they want, you will be able to get what you want. That's how it works.

Isn't it difficult to get your book published?

Technology has completely disrupted the publishing industry in the last few years.

It no longer takes years to write and publish a book. You don't even have to be concerned if anyone will ever accept your manuscript. In fact, you can be in control of every aspect of your book and have complete ownership of it.

You are the author of your life, and thanks to technology, in a matter of months you can go from an idea to the author of your book right from your kitchen table.

At the click of a button, your book can be available globally. Someone on the other side of the world can order your book from Amazon, Booktopia, Book Depository and numerous other platforms. You don't even have to go to the post office to send it. Transactions like these are happening millions of times a day.

What's your most inspiring client story?

It's hard to choose just one. I'm so fortunate to be able to assist others in creating a legacy that also becomes their business card and positions them as an expert. This means I've had a lot of success stories. In fact, I want everyone I work with to *become their own success story*, which is one of my taglines.

Hearing how someone got on a radio station they'd tried for six years to be featured on and were all of a sudden invited to appear after publishing their book, shows me the power of being a published author. Once they publish their books, many of my clients are featured on radio, national television, newspapers and magazines, have their books on shelves in bookstores, achieve number one bestseller status and are invited speakers.

I feel so proud each time I get a photo of a new author holding and *authorgraphing* their very first book that's in physical book stores sitting next to those of well-known authors or getting to experience how they're *sharing their message, making a difference and leaving a legacy*™.

What would you like your legacy be?

I love the concept of legacy, and it's absolutely one of the main reasons I feel compelled to help people write and publish their books, which are stored as a record in the national and state libraries of Australia, as well as obviously being in print. For your message or story to remain long after you've gone is an amazing gift. In some way I also want my legacy to be bigger than that, and although it's yet to materialise, I see my legacy as an orphanage, school or library that would outlive me.

I've always had books in my life, and I want all children to experience being able to hold one and read it.

My daughter authored her own children's book when she was eleven, called *Pandora and the Perfect Egg.* It's available in print and eBook everywhere and has also been donated and distributed to the following organisations: Books for PNG kids, The Gold Coast University Hospital children's ward as part of their get well bags, The Smith Family, The Royal Children's Hospital Brisbane, Balinese children and the Sunrise of Africa School in Kenya.

Seeing children's faces light up while repeating the lines and recognising how producing a book can give so much joy to others, is beyond words.

So in a way we're already playing a small role in creating a legacy.

Why is mindset important?

After interviewing over a hundred people for my *Millionaire* book series, I realised the common factor to their success was that they'd mastered their mindset. Without the right mindset, you're going to stop at the first obstacle that pops up in your path.

You can join a free twenty-one day Millionaire Mindset Challenge at *www.themillionaireschool.com* to get started. Remember, your mind is like a muscle, and just like when you want to be in peak performance, you don't go to the gym once and it's done. It's about constant and never-ending improvement.

I live on acreage, and one of my favourite things to do is to get on the tractor for hours at a time and listen to podcasts, audio recordings and audiobooks. Same for driving and exercising. Chose something you love to do and add some mind food to your workout. It will be more enriching than a good beat.

One of the practices I love, and have heard from several mentors, is the power of words and vibration. What you say after the words **I AM** is a powerful message to your subconscious brain. Statements such as I AM perfect health, successful, capable, kind, compassionate, wealthy and happy, will instruct your brain to get in tune with your words.

Stating I AM sick, tired, lazy, no good, hopeless, not good enough, not smart enough, pretty enough or experienced enough will ensure you bring more of what you don't want into your life.

When you elevate your thoughts, you elevate your success.

What are some of your biggest life lessons?

You're the author of your own life. It's absolutely up to you, and no one else, to write your own life story. You have to take a hundred percent responsibility. You can't blame other people, the government, the economy or any other made-up excuse for something that's happened to you. You're in control of your thoughts, and you have a choice in every single moment as to how you will view any situation in your life.

Choosing to live in the present moment is a great practice. If you're not in the moment, then you're in worry and fear of the future, which mostly consists of events that will never happen, or guilt and shame over situations that have happened in the past you can't change. It's a total waste of energy and robs you of living your life in the moment, which really is the only moment you're given.

Understand that everything that's happened to you up until this point in your life has led you to exactly where you need to be. Take time to be grateful for everything that's happened, even events you perceived as difficult at the time, and know it's part of who you needed to become to live your next chapter. Everything is moving you toward living the fullest expression of the life you're here to live.

> "Life is happening for you, not to you."
> ~ Tony Robbins

How can someone get on the Success Express?

I like to look at this in three parts: mind, body and spirit. All three components need to work together.

You need your body to take the actions that will take you on your journey. Without physical action, nothing happens.

Your mind will be put to use coming up with ways to order and organise your knowledge and the best ways to serve others.

The last part is the spirit, and it's all about INSPIRATION (in-spirit), such as when an idea comes to you, and you get goose bumps. Maybe you feel the urge to Google an idea or attend someone's workshop.

It's about the energy of the universe that's exists in everything that's inside and outside of you. I believe it's our job in life to stay connected with this energy or Source. When you're connected to it, you get a feeling like you're in flow, and everything in your life just seems simple and easy. Some call this luck. When you're not connected to Source, then situations can seem to go wrong and feel difficult.

I know when I become disconnected and focus on the negative, it's my work to get connected again. I'm fortunate that I've created my life surrounded by nature on my thirteen acre property that's also not far from the beach. It means being immersed in nature on a daily basis, even if it means picking up horse poo.

Practising yoga and meditation, walking on the beach or in nature, riding your bike and listening to music you love can be great ways to reconnect and instantly feel better. Nature has a high vibration, so it's really about vibrating at a high level.

There's some great information in a book called *Power Versus Force* by David Hawkins. Beware! It's heavy reading, but Google it, and you'll find great summaries. Basically, the message is that love and fulfilment and living your best life exist at a high level of vibration, and depression is at a low level. It's all about aligning your energy or vibration with the energy of the universe.

This is when you *Elevate Your Success*.

I will sign off this chapter with my all-time favourite quote that sums up the journey of a PassionPreneur.

> "Success is not the key to happiness. Happiness is the key to success. If you love what you are doing, you will be successful."
> ~Albert Schweitzer

 To discover more about how Fiona can help you *Elevate Your Success*, visit www.elevate-books.com/success

Ed Ng

Marketing To Millions

Ed Ng is a marketer, educator, speaker, published bestselling author and the founder of Marketing Synergy, a company that assists and teaches business owners how to incorporate ethical marketing and integrity into their selling practices.

Since 2007, he's created and overseen digital marketing strategies for various international businesses ranging from retail chains to e-commerce stores, as well as providing competitive services to leading authority blogs. He loves travelling and volunteers for not-for-profit organisations that support the environment, arts, youth, community and sustainability.

Having worked with and been mentored by influential masterminds in the mindset, business, marketing and internet worlds, Ed delivers proven strategies to his clients to help them share their message. If you'd like more information, please visit marketingsynergy.com.

Ed Ng
Marketing To Millions

Why is sharing about how to achieve successful marketing important to you?

As of right now, I've been in the industry for ten years. I'm a big believer in practising what you preach and putting words into action.

I've seen companies that have closed down due to poor marketing and sales techniques. In my business, Marketing Synergy, I strive to demonstrate the fundamental principles that underlay all businesses. Regardless of the industry you're in, all businesses are based on people looking for solutions. Your customers are human beings with emotions, needs, wants, fears and desires.

I've constantly witnessed marketing, particularly online marketing, refer to customers as clicks, statistics, data, dollar signs, conversion rates and impressions. Basically a lot of numbers and figures, since that's what the marketer or account manager looks at every day.

I wanted to return full circle to marketing's fundamental origins and for my company to bring the humanity back into it. At the end of the day, business is about providing services and products to help people overcome problems, objections and issues and to elevate them to the next level, so they can improve their current situation.

When I explain this to people, they comment on how much of a revolutionary concept it is. From where I stand, I believe this is what marketing should be, because that's where it stemmed from.

The key aspects I focus on in my marketing methods are based on my professional experiences over the years. These include:

- valuing your customers

- making sure the message you're communicating to your customers is aligned with the marketing

- being connected to the people, not the dollar

- making decisions based on statistics and data, not from hunches and emotional responses

- leveraging yourself.

I'm passionate about helping business owners build sustainable businesses, so they're able to grow them to their fullest potential, and in turn have the products and services they provide help their customers also live to their fullest potential.

How did you decide on the name and logo for your business, and how does it relate to your unique approach to marketing?

The name of my business, Marketing Synergy, came easily to me, as I wanted the branding to reflect my marketing principles. I believe there's a journey visitors go through when they come to a website and become long-term customers. I also believe in valuing the relationship a business has with its clients, which in turn creates reciprocity.

I have a holistic approach to marketing and a knack for explaining complicated concepts in simple terms. I love sharing my marketing concepts with my clients, watching them be applied and hearing their marketing success stories.

My approach is one that values people and respects the marketing fundamentals and principles. I wanted to demonstrate the synergistic relationship that marketing elements have with each other, so my logo is a five-piece Yin-Yang-looking symbol that represents five of the core areas of marketing I teach and implement for business owners. These are:

- search engine marketing (SEM)
- search engine optimisation (SEO)
- social media optimisation (SMO)
- site optimisation
- sales funnel optimisation (SFO)

The first three components are integral for generating visitors to a website, while the last two are aspects all business owners should utilise in the site's backend to increase their revenue.

Through my courses, I demonstrate how to get each of these marketing elements working together in synergy to turn your business website from an online brochure to a well-oiled marketing machine that will grow businesses and become more profitable, sustainable and highly leveraged.

Why is there a need for marketing to be successful?

Every business needs marketing to attract potential customers to their door, be it offline or online. A business needs constant "foot traffic" to be able to convert these prospects into clients through its sales funnel or process and bring revenue into the business.

All businesses need revenue in order to fund the overhead for the day-to-day operations, reinvest back into the marketing budget, save up for future projects and create a financial buffer in case of any unexpected emergencies.

Many business owners fail within the first five years, because they haven't set their marketing foundations right. It's not only important to have successful marketing strategies in place that bring in new customers every day but also to make sure these campaigns are representing you and your business accurately and honestly to the public.

You want to make sure that whatever products and services you provide do exactly what you state they do. Misrepresenting yourself through dishonest marketing tactics will tarnish your brand and goodwill, and these are both hard to get back once you've broken that trust.

Successful marketing campaigns not only create new clients but also raving fans who are genuinely willing to give you feedback, testimonials, referrals and great reviews to improve your business, network size and increase your customer base.

What's the first element to get right in marketing?

Always start with the end in mind. What's your goal and what do you hope to achieve? Then reverse engineer the steps required to achieve that goal. Is it to create revenue or increase your subscription, your checkout order size or brand visibility?

I've seen many marketing campaigns launched and operate without a clear direction towards their business outcome. Marketing can consume one of two critical resources: time or money. And sometimes both. So having a clear marketing plan is integral.

Is it necessary to have a business or marketing plan?

Having a plan or guideline is better than having none at all. But it's important to have a business model to support that plan. The purpose of using a model is to illustrate how all of the components of the business work together, such as:

- the content, products or services you're going to be delivering
- where the potential customers are going to come from
- how these people are going to be converted into paying customers
- what your plans are for the future of your business

Spending time to map out a business plan would be redundant if you didn't have a marketing plan to drive interested people to your business. They work hand in hand. What's the point in having a product or service, if you don't have anyone to market to, and no one is buying from you?

Have a clear path as to how you intend to bring potential clients, leads and customers into your business and present your offer to them.

Is it worth it to pay someone to do your marketing plan?

Paying a marketing or digital agency might save you time in figuring out all of the marketing complexities that go into researching, creating, launching, testing, monitoring, analysing and evaluating a campaign, but it does cost money.

You can also learn to market yourself through a course or program, but it takes time to learn and apply your marketing know-how. You might make some costly mistakes in your campaign if you don't set it up correctly. If you're going to learn marketing, I recommend you devote time to educating yourself about the policies and recommended practices for each of the advertising platforms you'll want to use.

There's nothing worse than putting time into researching and creating a campaign, only to launch it and have your ads disapproved, because they didn't comply with the platform's policies and procedures. Not getting your ads compliant the first time round will delay the running of your campaign. In the worst-case scenario, repeat offences may result in the platform getting banned or access to your account being blocked, effectively shutting down your advertising channel.

Thanks to technology, the world of marketing is constantly changing, and you will need to continue to invest time to stay on top of the latest updates from Google, Facebook and the multitude of social media platforms being released on a daily basis.

Overall, businesses rise and fall mainly due to two important factors, these being:

- *marketing*: the ability to get people to approach your business
- *sales*: the ability to make an exchange with people who interact with your business and translating that into revenue

Whether you're delegating your marketing to an agency or your in-house marketing department, marketing assistant or intern, in the end it's still your responsibility.

Take ownership of your marketing and make sure you communicate your goals effectively to whoever you're delegating to. No one knows your business and its products and services as well as you do, so ensure your team is on the same page and are onboard with your vision.

Why is it important to make marketing a priority?

I continually encounter people who want to be in business but don't want to be responsible for the marketing of it. That's a dangerous attitude to have that can ultimately end all of your business operations.

You need to be able to communicate effectively to your marketing team, whether in-house or outsourced, so you can bring to light the benefits and features of your product or service to your marketplace. Here are some questions that can assist in communicating effectively with your marketing team:

- What is your marketing goal?
- What is the result you want from your marketing campaign?
- How do you want to communicate with your marketplace?
- How do you want to communicate your branding, products, services and you as an individual?
- How do you want to be represented to the public?

Share your answers with your marketing team, so they can be on the same page, and continue to be in regular communications with them to hold them accountable.

Is it necessary to take marketing courses or become an expert in order to be successful in marketing?

Everyone's situation is different. However, in general, I believe it's crucial to have a good grasp of marketing, which is why I provide marketing courses and training for business owners and their teams.

Learning about marketing means business owners can immediately implement marketing principles into their business, teach these skills to their assistants or ensure they're not being ripped off by an employee or an outsourced marketing agency applying unscrupulous marketing practices.

Whether you're seeking out a marketing course, a marketing mentorship or a marketing degree, you should ask yourself the following questions:

- Is the content relevant to the current market situation?
- Do I have the time to invest and absorb the teachings?
- Will I apply what I've learnt into my business, so I'm able to make back the money I invested?

A business owner would require some discipline to be able to manage a business and its day-to-day operations, on top of absorbing and applying what they've learned. But it's worth it, as overall, you'll add more value to your business.

How important is it to have a website?

In today's competitive and digitally inclined world, it's important to have a website for your business to be visible and searchable online. However, it's even more important to make sure your website is a marketing tool promoting your business and not just an online brochure, so that it's working towards bringing you new potential clients.

Now that most businesses are online, is it still possible to get noticed on the internet?

While many businesses are online these days, not every website is optimised properly to be searchable by the search engines or user-friendly for visitors. Make sure your website is mobile-friendly, not just mobile-responsive. This means your site doesn't just fit across multiple devices, like mobile, tablet and desktop, but is also practical and functional for the user viewing it through these devices.

Making your website easy to navigate, adding relevant content and having a well optimised website are ways that you can boost your website's marketing performance and beat out your competitors.

Get to know your audience well. There may be other websites online that are in similar industries, talking about similar topics, but they don't have your business's community. The more you're in touch with your community, the more relevant and beneficial your online audience's experience will be. They become more responsive and may advocate your business to people they know.

What are the important elements that should be included on business websites?

A business website needs to instil value and trustworthiness. Today's website visitors are generally well-informed and suspicious, so you want to resonate trust.

Make sure you include trust seals, such as any relevant awards you've received and media you've been featured in, and include your branding on your website, such as your logo and tagline. Also be sure to have a clear call to action for visitors to take the next step with you, be that an opt-in box, phone number or contact form.

Sometimes it can be difficult for your potential customers to find the next course of action. I had a client, a photographer, who once asked me to review his website after he'd paid an SEO specialist to update his layout to be more SEO-friendly and mobile-responsive but discovered he was receiving fewer phone inquiries for bookings.

While the website was aesthetically pleasing, it wasn't user-friendly. One of the reasons why the new website version was performing poorly was that the phone number, one of the primary ways he generated business, was sitting on the bottom of his website, whereas his old version had the phone number visible on the top. It was an easy fix and could be applied to being viewed on multiple devices.

In a nutshell, remember to put your best foot forward and have a clear way for your potential clients to start working with you.

Should there be social media accounts across all of the major platforms?

Managing multiple social media platforms can be a handful without a system, such as a social management software or having a social media manager you can delegate the task to.

There are a myriad of social media platforms on the internet right now, and more are being created every day. However, your target audience may not be spending time on all of them. It's better to focus on a selection of social media platforms that contain the largest group of your target audience and provide quality engagement with the communities via these platforms.

What do successful marketing campaigns look like?

Successful marketing campaigns are able to communicate to their target market effectively, are able to bring new visitors to the website and convert these visitors into customers. The revenue generated from your sales is able to cover the marketing expenses and produce a profit that can be reinvested back into the marketing campaign to produce even more revenue.

Remember, not every visitor to your website will become a customer on day one of meeting you and your business. Those who don't convert are people who need more information in order to build trust.

Even though some visitors may not make a purchase or sign a deal on the spot, that doesn't mean that they won't consider coming onboard at a later date. You should continue to nurture a relationship with these prospects.

What's the best thing about successful marketing?

Once you've identified what's working in your campaign, you can easily duplicate your success and make a template based on what's been working well, then rinse and repeat the process for more predictable results in order to effectively streamline your marketing. In this case, you'll only be spending your marketing budget on what's been proven to work within your target market and minimise the spending on what doesn't.

Successful marketing allows you to create profits and reinvest them back into your marketing, which creates buffers for unforeseen emergencies, starting new projects and fundamentally building a sustainable business as you create marketing pipelines that work for you, rather than you working on it.

What's the biggest mistake businesses make in their marketing?

The biggest mistake, besides marketing without knowing their end goal, is not knowing their numbers and making marketing decisions based on hunches rather than facts.

Having tracking in place to measure your campaign's performance is vital. With tracking, not only can you see how many people are coming to your website but also how many of them are converting and responding to your site's call to action. These are figures that marketers need to know in order to evaluate a campaign's progress.

Using an analytic platform allows you to track data such as the visitors coming through the sales funnel and the sales being made, in order to accurately make decisions about your marketing campaigns, otherwise you're stabbing in the dark. Without tracking, you could be making marketing decisions based on emotions and inclinations and not the entire picture.

One of the biggest misconceptions with marketing, particularly with people who outsource it, is that marketing is simply flicking a switch on and off. The reality is there's no single magic button or silver bullet. Success in marketing comes from ongoing trial and error. It's all about testing the market, getting feedback, and adjusting and fine-tuning the campaign as you go.

How should marketing be tailored to the business?

In terms of tailoring marketing for your business, try to bring it back to what's in your marketplace. Before you create a product or service, ask your target market what they want and deliver it through marketing strategies based on their preferred method of communication and not the other way around.

The more in touch you are with your clients and customers and nurture these relationships, the more you lend yourself to forming a community of fans that love your products and services. You should always have your community's best interest at heart. Be their best friend, the expert on the subject and the authority of your niche and industry. In this way, the suggestions and recommendations you share with your community is appreciated as information that will benefit, serve and make their current situation better, because you're like a trusted friend.

The more you're able to communicate and have an open dialogue with your community, the more you get to uncover what it is they want, common situations they've experienced that you haven't yet addressed, how they found your products and services, and other areas of improvement. By asking your community the right questions, and you will be able to extract data and feedback that will benefit and improve your business.

How should businesses be promoted to a target audience?

If you're going to promote your business, product or service, do it in the mode that's most responsive to your target market. People learn and receive communications through various means. There's no one size fits all.

To explain this point further, I'm going to be referring to *VARK*, which is a learning system based around the findings of Neil Fleming, a New Zealand teacher who observed various learning behaviours in classrooms all over the country.

- **V**isual

    Graphs, charts, diagrams and symbols

- **A**uditory

    Lectures, discussions and podcasts

- **R**eading

    Text-based, blog articles and note taking

▶ **K**inesthetic

Feeling, touching and hands-on experiences

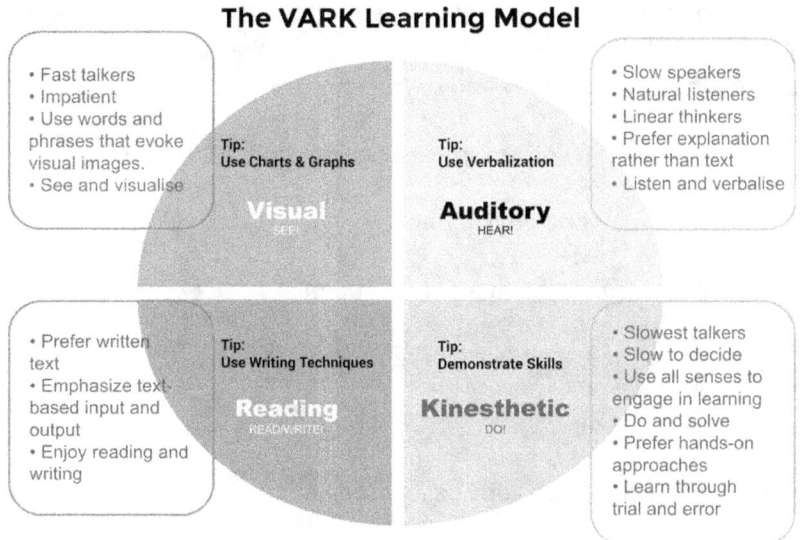

Whatever the marketing material or content you're creating, make sure the medium is most engaging to your specific target market. If you don't know, ask your community. Do they want images, diagrams, sound files, audio books, podcasts or text-based reading, or do they prefer a more hands-on, experiential approach?

Your marketing messages should appeal to the majority of your target audience, because it taps into their most preferred method. However, if you want to penetrate the marketplace deeper to get a larger share of the market, what you should do is create different marketing materials based on all of the different modes of learning, because you should aim to engage with everyone in your target market.

How can marketing be done successfully?

One way to be successful in marketing is to model it based on profitable companies in your industry. Stand on the shoulders of giants, so to speak, and investigate what they did in their campaigns to see if it applies to your business. They've already gone through the minefields of the marketplace, so learn from their mistakes and successes and save yourself time, money and resources.

Here are some of my other tips to be successful in marketing:

- Start with the end goal in mind.
- Research your target market thoroughly.
- Track and measure your marketing campaigns.
- Evaluate the results.
- Make business decisions based on data.
- Optimise if necessary.
- Continue with what works and cut out what doesn't.
- Put budget aside to explore being an early adopter of new technologies and innovation.

Testing newly released marketing channels does require time and money. However, if you can learn the ropes fast, you can beat your competitors by establishing your marketing presence before they jump onboard.

What if the marketing campaign isn't performing the way you want it to?

If you're running a marketing campaign that isn't converting, I suggest you pause it to prevent further monetary losses. Investigate, analyse, fix and optimise any campaign changes needed based on the data you've collected, before resuming the campaign.

When evaluating your campaigns, use this checklist:

1. State the marketing goal you wanted to achieve. Always have your goal in mind when evaluating whether your campaign is converting well.

2. Define the results that suggest the campaign isn't working for you, such as it not meeting your goal.

3. Take a look at the way you're communicating your promotion. Have a look at the text in the ads, if you're using them, and see if there are any discrepancies in communication, such as a discrepancy between the ad your visitors click on versus the landing page.

4. Check the landing page itself. Is it user friendly? Is the call to action visible? Visitors need to know how to take the next step.

5. Have at look at the site's functionality on the landing page, like whether the call to action buttons are working, if there are any issues with the checkout processes and if the links are working.

6. Check if your fulfilment processes are operational. If you have them, are the follow-up email sequences working? For instance, sending an invoice and dispatching fulfilment requests. Is your payment gateway or collection process method able to collect payments?

7. Most importantly, make sure all of your activities are being tracked, whether you're using Google Analytics, which I recommend because it integrates nicely with other Google applications, or some other tracking platform.

One key fact to remember about marking is to diversify the ways in which you're bringing visitors to your website, as well as your customer base. This way, you'll always have different options for marketing and revenue generation available to you in case any unpredictable changes to your business occur in the future.

Could you give one final tip about marketing successfully?

I trust you've received value from what I've shared of my fundamentals and principles to successful marketing. I've covered a lot of content, and I hope you'll be able to implement some of the key takeaways into your business immediately and get sustainable marketing results.

I've put together some of my best tips for business owners just like you in an exclusive marketing toolkit I've created. To find out more, please visit the link below where I demonstrate clear pathways for growing your business sustainably with successful marketing.

 To discover more about how Ed can help you *Elevate Your Success*, visit

www.elevate-books.com/success

Afterword

While you were reading these people's inspiring stories, did you notice something? All of their life experiences were for a purpose, bringing them closer to their goals, relationships and especially the message they were meant to share with the world.

The last page is a blank canvas for you to write the next chapter of your own story about elevating your success and inspiring others. Every day is a brand-new opportunity to be the author of your destiny.

Next Steps

To support you on your journey to *Elevate Your Success*, we recommend you take advantage of these resources:

7 Day Transformation Program

To join this 7-day transformation online program, simply go to: www.elevate-books.com/you

👥 Connect with the Authors

To discover more about the authors and what they have to teach you, and bonus gifts they are offering visit: www.elevate-books.com/success

🎙 Subscribe to our Podcast

If you'd like to hear the go-to interviews from the authors and be re-inspired, check out: www.elevate-books.com/podcast

🌐 Visit the Website

To find out more about the Elevate book series, visit: www.elevate-books.com

www.ingramcontent.com/pod-product-compliance
Lightning Source LLC
Chambersburg PA
CBHW071233080526
44587CB00013BA/1590